C000228705

Бжⷭ҇твеннам лїтꙋргі́а
и҆́же во ст҃ы́хъ ѻ҆тца̀ на́шегѡ і҆ѡа́нна златоꙋ́стагѡ

The Divine Liturgy
of Our Father among the Saints
John Chrysostom

И҆зда́тельство
Свѧто-Тро́ицкагѡ монастырѧ.
Тѷпогра́фїѧ преп. І҆́ѡва Поча́евскагѡ.
Джорданви́лль, Н.І́.

Printed with the blessing of His Eminence,
Metropolitan Hilarion, First Hierarch of the
Russian Orthodox Church Outside of Russia

The Divine Liturgy of Our Father Among the Saints
John Chrysostom: Slavonic-English Parallel Text
© 1985, 1987, 2013 Holy Trinity Monastery,
Fourth edition 2015
Second Printing 2019
Fifth Edition 2022

PRINTSHOP OF SAINT JOB OF POCHAEV

An imprint of

HOLY TRINITY PUBLICATIONS
Holy Trinity Monastery
Jordanville, New York 13361-0036
www.holytrinitypublications.com

ISBN: 978-0-884645-484-1

Library of Congress Control Number 2015942853

All rights reserved.
Printed in the China

Table of Contents

Чинъ
Бжественныя літургіи
йже во стыхъ
Отца нашегw
Іwанна Златоустагw

Тисненіе пятое

The Order
of
The Divine Liturgy
of
Our Father Among the Saints
John Chrysostom

FIFTH EDITION

Бжⷭ҇твеннаѧ літꙋргі́а
иже во стыхъ ѻ҆тца̀ на́шегѡ
і҆ѡа́нна златоꙋстагѡ

Проскомі́дїа

Хотѧ́й сще́нникъ бжⷭ҇твенное
соверша́ти тайнодѣ́йствїе, до́лженъ
є҆́сть пе́рвѣе ᲂу҆́бѡ примире́нъ бы́ти
со всѣ́ми, и҆ не и҆мѣ́ти что̀ на кого̀,
и҆ се́рдце же, є҆ли́ка си́ла, ѿ лꙋка́выхъ
блюстѝ помыслѡ́въ, воздержа́тисѧ же
съ ве́чера, и҆ трезви́тисѧ да́же до вре́мене
сщеннодѣ́йствїѧ. Вре́мени же наста́вшꙋ,
вхо́дитъ въ хра́мъ и҆ соедни́всѧ со
дїа́кономъ, творѧ́тъ вкꙋ́пѣ къ восто́кꙋ
пред сты́ми две́рьми поклоне́нїѧ трѝ.

The Divine Liturgy of Our Father among the Saints John Chrysostom

The Proskomedia

The priest that desires to celebrate the Divine Mysteries must first be at peace with all, having nothing against anyone, and insofar as is within his power, keep his heart from evil thoughts, be continent from the evening before, and be vigilant until the time of the divine service. When the time is come, he goes into the church, together with the deacon, and together they make three bows to the waist towards the east before the holy doors.

Та́же глаго́летъ діа́конъ: Блгослови̏, влады́ко.

Сще́нникъ: Блгослове́нъ бгъ на́шъ всегда̀, ны́нѣ и при́снw, и во вѣ́ки вѣкẃвъ. А҆ми́нь.

Начина́етъ глаго́лати діа́конъ: Цр҃ю̀ нбсный: Трист҃о́е. По Оч҃е на́шъ:

Сще́нникъ: Ꙗ҆́кw твоѐ є҆́сть цртво:

Та́же глаго́лютъ: Поми́луй на́съ, гд҃и, поми́луй на́съ: всѧ́кагw бо ѿвѣ́та недоумѣ́юще, сію̀ тѝ млтву ꙗ҆́кw влцѣ грѣ́шніи прино́симъ: поми́луй на́съ.

Сла́ва: Гд҃и, поми́луй на́съ, на тѧ́ бо оу҆пова́хомъ, не прогнѣ́вайсѧ на ны̀ ѕѣлẁ, нижѐ помѧнѝ беззако́ній на́шихъ: но при́зри и ны́нѣ ꙗ҆́кw блгоутро́бенъ, и и҆зба́ви ны̀ ѿ вра́гъ на́шихъ: ты́ бо є҆сѝ бг҃ъ на́шъ, и мы̀ лю́діе твоѝ, всѝ дѣла̀ руку̀ твоє́ю, и и҆́мѧ твоѐ призыва́емъ.

Deacon: Bless, master.
Priest: Blessed is our God, always, now and ever, and unto the ages of ages. Amen.

The deacon begins: O Heavenly King…
Trisagion to Our Father…

Priest: For Thine is the kingdom…
Then they say: Have mercy on us, O Lord, have mercy on us, for at a loss for any defence, this prayer do we sinners offer unto Thee as Master: have mercy on us.

Glory…Lord, have mercy on us, for we have hoped in Thee. Be not angry with us greatly, neither remember our iniquities; but look upon us now as Thou art compassionate, and deliver us from our enemies; for Thou art our God, and we, Thy people; all are the works of Thy hands, and we call upon thy name.

И҆ ны́нѣ: Ми́лⷭⷣрдїѧ две́ри ѿве́рзи на́мъ, блгⷭⷵове́ннаѧ бцⷣе, надѣ́ющїисѧ на тѧ̀ да не поги́бнемъ, но да и҆зба́вимсѧ тобо́ю ѿ бѣ́дъ, ты́ бо є҆сѝ спⷵнїе ро́да хрⷵтїа́нскагѡ.

Та́же ѿхо́дѧтъ ко і҆кѡ́нѣ хрⷵто́вѣ и҆ цѣлꙋ́ютъ ю̀, глаго́люще:

Пречⷵтомꙋ твоемꙋ̀ ѻ҆́бразꙋ покланѧ́емсѧ бл҃гі́й, просѧ́ще проще́нїѧ прегрѣше́нїй на́шихъ, хрⷵтѐ бж҃е: во́лею бо бл҃говоли́лъ є҆сѝ пло́тїю взы́ти на крⷵтъ, да и҆зба́виши, ꙗ҆́же созда́лъ є҆сѝ, ѿ рабо́ты вра́жїѧ, тѣ́мъ бл҃года́рственнѡ вопїе́мъ тѝ: ра́дости и҆спо́лнилъ є҆сѝ всѧ̑ спⷵе на́шъ, прише́дый спⷵтѝ мі́ръ.

Та́же цѣлꙋ́ютъ и҆ і҆кѡ́нꙋ бцⷣы глаго́люще тропа́рь:

Both now…Open unto us the doors of compassion, O blessed Theotokos, for, hoping in thee, may we not perish, through thee may we be delivered from adversities, for thou art the salvation of the Christian race.

Then they approach the icon of Christ and kiss it, saying:

We worship Thine immaculate Icon, O Good One, asking the forgiveness of our failings, O Christ God; for of Thine own will Thou wast well-pleased to ascend the Cross in the flesh, that Thou mightest deliver from slavery to the enemy those whom Thou hadst fashioned. Wherefore, we cry to Thee thankfully: Thou didst fill all things with joy, O our Saviour, when Thou camest to save the world.

Then they kiss the icon of the Theotokos, saying the troparion:

Ма́рдїа су́щи исто́чникъ, ма́ти сподо́би на́съ, бц҃е, при́зри на лю́ди согрѣши́вшыа, і҆ави́ і҆ако прⷭнѡ си́лꙋ твою̀, на та̀ бо ᲂу҆пова́юще, ра́дꙋйса вопїе́мъ тѝ, і҆акоже и҆ногда̀ гаврїи́лъ, безпло́тныхъ а҆рхїстрати́гъ.

Та́же приклⷩь главꙋ̀, і҆ере́й глаго́летъ:

Гдⷭи, низпосли́ рꙋ́кꙋ твою̀ съ высоты̀ ст҃а́гѡ жили́ща твоегѡ̀, и҆ ᲂу҆крѣпи́ ма въ предлежа́щꙋю слꙋ́жбꙋ твою̀: да неѡсꙋ_ жде́ннѡ предста́нꙋ стра́шномꙋ прⷭто́лꙋ твоемꙋ̀, и҆ безкро́вное сщ҃еннодѣ́йствїе соверша̀. Ꙗ҆́кѡ твоа̀ є҆́сть си́ла и҆ сла́ва во вѣ́ки вѣкѡ́въ. А҆ми́нь.

Та́же творатъ и҆ къ ликѡ́мъ покло́ны по є҆ди́номъ: и҆ та́кѡ ѿхо́датъ въ же́ртвенникъ, глаголю́ще:

Вни́дꙋ въ до́мъ тво́й, поклоню́са ко хра́мꙋ ст҃о́мꙋ твоемꙋ̀ въ стра́сѣ твое́мъ. Гдⷭи, наста́ви ма пра́вдою твое́ю, вра́гъ мои́хъ

As thou art a well-spring of compassion, vouchsafe mercy unto us, O Theotokos. Look upon a sinful people; show forth, as always, thy power. For, hoping in thee, we cry 'Rejoice!' to thee, as once did Gabriel, the supreme commander of the bodiless hosts.

Then, with bowed head, the priest says:

O Lord, stretch forth Thy hand from Thy holy place on high, and strengthen me for this, Thine appointed service; that, standing uncondemned before Thy dread altar, I may celebrate the bloodless ministry. For Thine is the power and the glory unto the ages of ages. Amen.

Then they make a bow
to each choir, and go into
the altar, saying:

I will come into Thine house; in Thy fear will I worship toward Thy holy temple. Lead me, O Lord, in Thy righteousness; because of

ра́ди испра́ви пред тобо́ю пꙋ́ть мо́й. Ꙗ҆́кѡ
нѣ́сть во ѹ҆стѣ́хъ и҆́хъ и҆́стины, се́рдце и҆́хъ
сꙋ́етно, гро́бъ ѿве́рстъ горта́нь и҆́хъ, ѧ҆зы́ки
свои́ми льща́хꙋ. Сꙋди́ и҆̀мъ, бж҃е, да ѿпадꙋ́тъ
ѿ мы́слей свои́хъ: по мно́жествꙋ нече́стїѧ
и҆́хъ и҆зри́ни ѧ҆̀, ꙗ҆́кѡ преѡгорчи́ша тѧ̀, гдⷭ҇и.
И҆ да возвеселѧ́тсѧ всѝ ѹ҆пова́ющїи на тѧ̀,
во вѣ́къ возра́дꙋютсѧ, и҆ всели́шисѧ въ
ни́хъ: и҆ похва́лѧтсѧ ѡ҆ тебѣ̀ лю́бѧщїи и҆́мѧ
твоѐ. Ꙗ҆́кѡ ты̀ бл҃гослови́ши пра́ведника,
гдⷭ҇и, ꙗ҆́кѡ ѻ҆рꙋ́жїемъ бл҃говоле́нїѧ вѣнча́лъ
є҆сѝ на́съ.

Вше́дше же во ст҃и́лище, творѧ́тъ
покло́ны трѝ пред ст҃о́ю трапе́зою и҆
цѣлꙋ́ютъ ст҃о́е є҆ѵⷢ҇лїе и҆ ст҃ꙋ́ю трапе́зꙋ. Та́же
прїе́млютъ въ рꙋ́ки своѧ̀ кі́ждо стїха́рь
сво́й, и҆ творѧ́тъ покло́ны трѝ къ восто́кꙋ,
глаго́люще въ себѣ̀ кі́ждо:

mine enemies, make my way plain before Thee. For there is no truth in their mouth; their heart is vain; their throat is an open sepulcher; they flatter with their tongue. Judge them, O God; let them fall through their own imaginations; cast them out according to the multitude of their ungodliness; for they have embittered Thee, O Lord. And let all them that put their trust in Thee be glad; they shall ever rejoice; and Thou shalt dwell in them and they that love Thy name shall be joyful in Thee. For Thou wilt bless the righteous, O Lord, for with the shield of Thy favorable kindness hast Thou crowned us.

Having entered into the sanctuary, they make three prostrations before the Holy Table and kiss the Holy Gospel and the Holy Table. Then each one takes his sticharion in his hands, and they make three bows to the waist toward the east, while saying to themselves with each bow:

Бже, ѡчисти мѧ грѣшнаго и помилꙋй мѧ.

Та́же прихо́дитъ ко сщ҃е́ннику дїа́конъ, держа̀ въ деснѣ́й рꙋцѣ̀ стїха́рь со ѻрꙋре́мъ, и подклони́въ є҆мꙋ̀ главꙋ̀, глаго́летъ:

Бл҃гословѝ, влады́ко, стїха́рь со ѻрꙋре́мъ.

Сщ҃е́нникъ глаго́летъ:

Бл҃гослове́нъ бг҃ъ на́шъ всегда̀, ны́нѣ и при́снѡ и во вѣ́ки вѣкѡ́въ.

Та́же ѿхо́дитъ дїа́конъ во є҆ди́нꙋ странꙋ̀ стꙗ́лница, и ѡблача́итсѧ въ стїха́рь, молѧ́сѧ си́це:

Возра́дꙋетсѧ дꙋша̀ моѧ̀ ѡ гдⷭѣ, ѡблече́ бо мѧ̀ въ ри́зꙋ сп҃се́нїѧ, и ѻ҆де́ждею весе́лїѧ ѡдѣ́ѧ мѧ̀, ꙗ҆́кѡ жениху̀ возложи́ ми вѣне́цъ, и ꙗ҆́кѡ невѣ́стꙋ оу҆краси́ мѧ красото́ю.

O God, cleanse me a sinner and have mercy on me.

Then the deacon comes to the priest, holding in his right hand the sticharion with the orarion, and bowing his head before the priest, says:

Bless, master, the sticharion with the orarion.

The priest says:

Blessed is our God, always, now and ever, and unto the ages of ages.

Then the deacon goes to one side of the sanctuary, puts on the sticharion, praying in these words:

My soul shall rejoice in the Lord, for He hath clothed me in the garment of salvation, and with the vesture of gladness hath He covered me; He hath placed a crown upon me as on a bridegroom, and He hath adorned me as a bride with comeliness.

И҆ ѻ҆ра́рь ѹ҆́бѡ цѣлова́въ, налага́етъ на лѣ́вое ра́мо. Нарꙋка́вницы же налага́ѧ на рꙋ́ки, на деснꙋ́ю ѹ҆́бѡ, глаго́летъ:

Десни́ца твоѧ̀, гдⷭ҇и, просла́висѧ въ крѣ́пости: десна́ѧ твоѧ̀ рꙋка̀, гдⷭ҇и, сокрꙋшѝ врагѝ, и҆ мно́жествомъ сла́вы твоеѧ̀ стёрлъ є҆сѝ сꙋпоста́ты.

На лѣ́вꙋю же, глаго́летъ:

Рꙋ́цѣ твоѝ сотвори́стѣ мѧ̀ и҆ созда́стѣ мѧ̀: вразꙋмѝ мѧ, и҆ наꙋчꙋ́сѧ за́повѣдемъ твои̑мъ.

Та́же ѿше́дъ въ предложе́нїе, ѹ҆готовлѧ́етъ сщⷳе́ннаѧ. Ст҃ы́й ѹ҆́бѡ дїскосъ поставлѧ́етъ ѿ шꙋ́юю странꙋ̀, потира̀ же, є҆́же є҆́сть ст҃ꙋ́ю ча́шꙋ, ѿ деснꙋ́ю, и҆ про́чаѧ съ ни́ми.

Сщⷳе́нникъ же си́це ѡ҆блача́етсѧ: прїе́мь стїха́рь въ лѣ́вꙋю рꙋ́кꙋ, и҆ поклони́всѧ

And then kissing the orarion, he places it on
the left shoulder. Then putting the cuffs on
the hands, starting with the right cuff he says:

Thy right hand, O Lord, is become glorious in power; Thy right hand, O Lord,
hath dashed in pieces the enemy, and in the
abundance of Thy glory Thou hast wiped
out Thine adversaries.

And continuing with the left, he says:

Thy hands have made me and fashioned me;
O give me understanding, and I shall learn
Thy commandments.

Then, going to the Table of Oblation, he
prepares the holy vessels. He places the
holy diskos on the left side; the chalice, that
is, the holy cup, on the right; and the rest
(the spoon, spear, etc.) with them.

And the priest vests himself thus: taking
the sticharion in his left hand, and bowing
three times toward the east, as mentioned

трижды къ востокꙋ, ꙗкоже речеса,
назнаменꙋетъ, глаголꙗ:

Бл҃гословенъ бг҃ъ нашъ всегда, нн҃ѣ и
прⷭ҇нѡ, и во вѣки вѣкѡвъ. Амн҃ь.

Таже ѡблачитса, глаголꙗ:

Возрадꙋетса дꙋша моꙗ ѡ гдⷭ҇ѣ, ѡблече бо
ма въ ризꙋ сп҃сенїа, и одеждею веселїа
ѡдѣа ма, ꙗкѡ женихꙋ возложи ми
вѣнецъ, и ꙗкѡ невѣстꙋ оукраси ма
красотою.

Таже прїемъ епїтрахиль и назнаменавъ,
ѡблагаетса ею, глаголꙗ:

Бл҃гословенъ бг҃ъ изливаай бл҃годать свою
на сщ҃енники своꙗ ꙗкѡ мѵро на главѣ,
сходащее на брадꙋ, брадꙋ ааршⷭ҇ню, сходащее
на ѡметы одежди егѡ.

Таже прїемъ поꙗсъ и ѡпоасꙋꙗса,
глаголетъ:

before, he signs it with the sign of the
Cross, saying:

Blessed is our God, always, now and ever,
and unto the ages of ages. Amen.

Then he vests himself, saying:

My soul shall rejoice in the Lord, for He
hath clothed me in the garment of salvation,
and with the vesture of gladness hath He
covered me; He hath placed a crown upon
me as on a bridegroom and He hath adorned
me as a bride with comeliness.

Then taking the epitrachelion and signing
it, he puts it on, saying:

Blessed is God Who poureth out His grace
upon His priests, it is like the myrrh upon
the head, that runneth down upon the beard,
even Aaron's beard, and goeth down to the
fringes of his clothing.

Then taking the belt and girding himself,
he says:

Блгослове́нъ бг҃ъ препоѧсꙋ́ай мѧ си́лою, и҆ положѝ непоро́ченъ пꙋ́ть мо́й, соверша́ай но́зѣ моѝ ꙗ҆́кѡ є҆ле́ни, и҆ на высо́кихъ поставлѧ́ай мѧ̀.

Нарꙋка́вницы же, ꙗ҆́кѡ вы́ше рече́сѧ. Та́же прїе́мъ набе́дренникъ, а҆́ще и҆́мать, и҆ блгослови́въ и҆̀, и҆ цѣлова́въ, глаго́летъ:

Препоѧ́ши ме́чь тво́й по бедрѣ̀ твое́й, си́льне, красото́ю твое́ю и҆ добро́тою твое́ю, и҆ налѧцы̀, и҆ ᲂу҆спѣва́й, и҆ цр҃твꙋ́й, и҆́стины ра́ди и҆ кро́тости и҆ пра́вды, и҆ наста́витъ тѧ̀ ди́внѡ десни́ца твоѧ̀, всегда̀, ны́нѣ и҆ при́снѡ и҆ во вѣ́ки вѣкѡ́въ. А҆ми́нь.

Та́же прїе́мъ фелѡ́нь и҆ блгослови́въ, цѣлꙋ́етъ, глаго́лѧ си́це:

Сщ҃е́нницы твоѝ, гд҃и, ѡ҆блекꙋ́тсѧ въ пра́вдꙋ, и҆ преподо́бнїи твоѝ ра́достїю возра́дꙋютсѧ всегда̀, ны́нѣ и҆ при́снѡ и҆ во вѣ́ки вѣкѡ́въ. А҆ми́нь.

Blessed is God that hath girded me with strength, and made my way perfect, that maketh my feet like harts' feet, and setteth me up on high.

Then the cuffs, in the manner described. Then taking the epigonation, if he has it, and having blessed and kissed it, he says:

Gird Thy sword upon Thy thigh, O Thou most Mighty, according to Thy splendor and Thy beauty, and bend Thy bow, and prosper, and reign, for the sake of truth, and meekness, and righteousness; and Thy right hand shall guide Thee wonderfully, always, now and ever, and unto the ages of ages. Amen.

Then taking the phelonion, and having blessed and kissed it, he says:

Thy priests, O Lord, shall be clothed with righteousness, and Thy saints shall rejoice, always, now and ever, and unto the ages of ages. Amen.

Та́же ѿше́дше въ предложе́нїе, оу҆мыва́ютъ
ру́ки, глаго́лz:

Оу҆мы́ю въ непови́нныхъ ру́цѣ мои́, и҆ ѡ҆бы́ду
же́ртвенникъ тво́й, гдⷭ҇и, є҆́же оу҆слы́шати
ми гла́съ хвалы̀ твоеS, и҆ повѣ́дати всS
чудеса̀ твоS. Гдⷭ҇и, возлюби́хъ блгⷪ҇лѣ́пїе
до́му твоегѡ̀, и҆ мѣ́сто селе́нїz сла́вы
твоеS. Да не погуби́ши съ нечести́выми
ду́шу мою̀, и҆ съ му́жи крове́й живота̀
моегѡ̀: и҆́хже въ рука́хъ беззакѡ́нїz,
десни́ца и҆́хъ и҆спо́лнисz мзды̀. А҆́зъ же
неѕло́бїемъ мои́мъ ходи́хъ, и҆зба́ви мS,
гдⷭ҇и, и҆ поми́луй мS. Нога̀ моS ста̀ на
правотѣ̀, въ це́рквахъ блгⷭ҇ловлю̀ тS, гдⷭ҇и.

Та́же поклоне́нїz трѝ пред̾ предложе́нїемъ
сотво́рше, глаго́лютъ кі́йждо:

Бж҃е, ѡ҆чи́сти мS грѣ́шнаго и҆ поми́луй
мS. И҆: И҆скупи́лъ ны̀ є҆сѝ ѿ клźтвы
зако́нныz чⷭ҇тно́ю твое́ю кро́вїю: на

Then, having gone to the sacristy, they
wash their hands, saying:

I will wash my hands in innocency, O Lord,
and so will I go round about Thine altar;
That I may hear the voice of Thy praise,
and tell of all Thy wondrous works. Lord, I
have loved the beauty of Thy house, and the
dwelling-place of Thy glory. O destroy not
my soul with the ungodly, nor my life with
the blood-thirsty; in whose hand is wicked-
ness, and their right hand is full of bribes.
But as for me, I have walked innocently;
deliver me, O Lord, and have mercy on me.
My foot hath stood on the right; I will bless
thee, O Lord, in the churches.

Then making three bows to the waist
before the Table of Oblation, each says:

O God, cleanse me a sinner and have mercy
on me. And: Thou hast redeemed us from
the curse of the law by Thy precious Blood:

крⷭтѣ̀ пригвоздѝвсѧ и̑ копі́емъ прободе́сѧ,
безсме́ртїе и̑сточи́лъ є̑сѝ человѣ́кѡмъ:
спⷭе на́шъ, сла́ва тебѣ̀.

Та́же глаго́летъ дїа́конъ:

Бл҃гословѝ, влады́ко.

И̑ начина́етъ сщ҃е́нникъ:

Бл҃гослове́нъ бг҃ъ на́шъ всегда̀, ны́нѣ и̑
при́снѡ и̑ во вѣ́ки вѣкѡ́въ.
Дїа́конъ: А̑ми́нь.

Та́же прїе́млетъ сщ҃е́нникъ лѣ́вою оу҆́бѡ
руко́ю просфору̀, десно́ю же ст҃о́е копі́е,
и̑ зна́менуѧ и̑мъ три́жды верху̀ печа́ти
просфоры̀, глаго́летъ:

Въ воспомина́нїе гдⷭа и̑ бг҃а и̑ спⷭа на́шегѡ
і̑и҃са хрⷭта̀. Три́жды.

И̑ а҆́бїе водружа́етъ копі́е въ десну́ю страну̀
печа́ти, и̑ глаго́летъ рѣ́жа:

Ꙗ̑́кѡ о҆вча̀ на заколе́нїе веде́сѧ.

nailed to the Cross and pierced with a spear, Thou hast poured forth immortality upon mankind, O our Saviour, glory to Thee.

Then the deacon says:

Bless, master.

And the priest begins:

Blessed is our God, always, now and ever, and unto the ages of ages.
Deacon: Amen.

Then the priest takes a prosphora in his left hand, and in his right hand the holy spear, and making with it the sign of the cross thrice over the seal of the prosphora, he says:

In remembrance of our Lord and God and Saviour, Jesus Christ. Thrice.

And immediately he thrusts the spear into the right side of the seal, and cutting it, he says:

He was led as a sheep to the slaughter.

Въ лѣ́вꙋю же:

И҆ ꙗ҆́кѡ а҆́гнецъ непоро́ченъ, пря́мѡ стригꙋ́щагѡ є҆го̀ безгла́сенъ, та́кѡ не ѿверза́етъ оу҆́стъ свои́хъ.

Въ го́рнюю же странꙋ̀ печа́ти:

Во смире́нїи є҆гѡ̀ сꙋ́дъ є҆гѡ̀ взя́тсѧ.

Въ до́льнюю же странꙋ̀:

Ро́дъ же є҆гѡ̀ кто̀ и҆сповѣ́сть;

Дїа́конъ же взира́ѧ бл҃гоговѣ́йнѡ на сицево́е та́инство, глаго́летъ на є҆ди́нѣмъ ко́емждо рѣ́занїи:

Гдꙋ̀ помо́лимсѧ:

держа̀ и҆ ѻ҆ра́рь въ рꙋцѣ̀.
По си́хъ глаго́летъ:

Возмѝ, влады́ко.

Сщ҃е́нникъ же, вложи́въ ст҃о́е копїѐ ѿ ко́свенныѧ десны́ѧ страны̀ просфоры̀, взима́етъ ст҃ы́й хлѣ́бъ, глаго́лѧ си́це:

And into the left side:

And as a blameless lamb before his shearer is dumb, so He openeth not his mouth.

And into the upper side of the seal:

In His humiliation His judgment was taken away.

And into the lower side:

And who shall declare his generation?

And the deacon, gazing reverently at this Mystery, says at each of these incisions:

Let us pray to the Lord;

holding also his orarion in his hand. After this he says:

Take away, master.

And the priest, having thrust the holy spear obliquely into the right side of the prosphora, takes away the holy bread, saying thus:

Я́кw взе́млетсѧ ѿ земли́ живо́тъ є҆гẁ.

И҆ положи́въ и҆̀ взна́къ на ст҃е́мъ ді́скосѣ,
ре́кшꙋ дїа́конꙋ:

Пожрѝ, влады́ко.

Жре́тъ є҆го̀ крестови́днw,
си́це глаго́лѧ:

Жре́тсѧ а҆́гнецъ бж҃їй, взе́млѧй грѣ́хъ мі́ра,
за мі́рскїй живо́тъ и҆ сп҃се́нїе.

И҆ ѡ҆браща́етъ горѣ̀ дрꙋгꙋ́ю странꙋ̀,
и҆мꙋ́щꙋю крⷭ҇тъ.

Дїа́конъ глаго́летъ:

Прободѝ, влады́ко.

Сщ҃е́нникъ же, пробода́ѧ и҆̀ въ деснꙋ́ю странꙋ̀
копїе́мъ, глаго́летъ:

Є҆ди́нъ ѿ вои́нъ копїе́мъ ре́бра є҆гẁ
прободѐ, и҆ а҆́бїе и҆зы́де кро́вь и҆ вода̀: и҆

For His life is taken away from the earth.

And the priest having laid it inverted on
the holy diskos, the deacon says:

Sacrifice, master.

And he cuts it in the form of the Cross,
while saying:

Sacrificed is the Lamb of God that taketh
away the sin of the world, for the life and
salvation of the world.

And he turns upward the other side, which
has the sign of the Cross.

The deacon says:

Pierce, master.

And the priest, piercing also in the right
side with the spear, says:

One of the soldiers with a spear pierced His
side, and forthwith came there out blood and

ви́дѣвый свидѣ́тельствова, и и́стинно
є҆́сть свидѣ́тельство є҆гѡ̀.

Дїа́конъ же, прїе́мъ вїно̀ и во́дꙋ, глаго́летъ
ко сщ҃е́нникꙋ:

Блгословѝ, влады́ко, ст҃о́е соедине́нїе.

И҆ взе́мъ над ни́ми блгослове́нїе,
вливае́тъ во ст҃ы́й поти́ръ ѿ вина̀
вкꙋ́пѣ и҆ воды̀.

[Є҆гда̀ же и҆ въ проскомі́дїи і҆ере́й, глаго́ла
словеса̀ сїѧ̀: а҆́бїе и҆зы́де кро́вь и҆ вода̀, воды̀
ма́лѡ не влїе́тъ, є҆́ще же по ѡ҆сщ҃е́нїи
ст҃ы́хъ та́инъ во своѐ вре́мѧ, є҆гда̀ влага́етъ
во ст҃ы́й поти́ръ ча́сть ст҃а́гѡ а҆́гнца, не
влїе́тъ ма́лѡ те́плыѧ воды̀, и҆лѝ вмѣ́стѡ
те́плыѧ хла́днꙋю влїе́тъ во́дꙋ, сме́ртнѡ,
ꙗ҆́кѡ престꙋ́пникъ цр҃ко́внагѡ преда́нїѧ,
согрѣши́тъ.

water. And he that saw it bare witness, and his witness is true.

The deacon, taking wine and water, says to the priest:

Bless, master, the holy union.

And receiving the blessing upon them, he pours wine together with water into the holy chalice.

[If the priest, having said the following words: "**and forthwith came there out blood and water**", does not pour in a little water, and also if, after the consecration of the Holy Mysteries in its proper time, when he puts into the holy chalice a piece of the Holy Lamb, he does not pour in a little warm water, or instead of warm water pours cold water, he is committing a mortal sin as one who breaks a tradition of the Church.

Вливати же воду въ проскомідіи, или
по совершеніи во потиръ, должно съ
вѣлїнмъ тщанїемъ смотрѣти, ёже бы
вїну свойственнагш вкуса не измѣнити
въ водный: ибо тайна въ сицевомъ вїнѣ,
ёже во вкусѣ водный измѣнится, не
совершится, и служай тяжкш смертню
согрѣшитъ.]

The Holy Bread
That is the Lamb

The Most Holy Theotokos

Ranks

The Living

The Dead

When the priest pours the water into the chalice during the Proskomedia, or after the consecration, he must with great care be sure that the wine does not lose its natural taste and begin tasting like water: for in such wine, when its taste changes to that of water, the Mystery shall not be celebrated, and the celebrant shall commit a mortal sin.]

Сщенникъ, прїемъ въ рꙋцѣ вторꙋю
просфорꙋ, глаголетъ:

Въ честь и память пребл҃гословенныѧ
вл҃чцы нашеѧ бц҃ы и приснодѣвы мр҃їи,
єѧже молитвами прїимѝ, гд҃и, жертвꙋ
сїю въ пренбⷭ҇ный твой жертвенникъ.

И вземъ частицꙋ, полагаетъ ю̀
ѡдеснꙋю ст҃агѡ хлѣба, близъ среды̀
єгѡ̀, глаголѧ:

Предста̀ цр҃ица ѡдеснꙋю тебѐ, въ ризы
позлащенны ѡдѣѧна, преꙋкрашенна.

Тѣже прїемъ третїю просфорꙋ, глаголетъ:

Честнагѡ славнагѡ прⷪ҇рока, прⷣ҇течи и
крⷭ҇тителѧ іѡанна.

И вземъ первꙋю частицꙋ, полагаетъ ю̀ ѡ
шꙋюю странꙋ ст҃агѡ хлѣба, творѧ начало
перваго чина.

The priest, taking in his hand the second prosphora, says:

In honor and remembrance of our most blessed Lady, the Theotokos and Ever-Virgin Mary, through whose intercessions do Thou, O Lord, receive this sacrifice upon Thy most heavenly altar.

And taking out a particle, he places it on the right side of the holy bread, near its middle, saying:

Upon Thy right hand did stand the Queen, in garments of gold is she vested, wrought about with divers colors.

Then taking the third prosphora, he says:

Of the honorable glorious Prophet, Fore-runner, and Baptist John.

And taking out the first particle, he places it on the left side of the holy bread, making the beginning of the first row.

Та́же глаго́летъ:

Ст҃ы́хъ сла́вныхъ прⷬ҇ро́кѡвъ: мѡѷсе́а и аарѡ́на, и҆лїи̑, и҆ є҆лїссе́а, дв҃да и҆ і҆ессе́а: ст҃ы́хъ трїе́хъ ѻ҆трокѡ́въ, и҆ данїи́ла прⷬ҇ро́ка, и҆ всѣ́хъ ст҃ы́хъ прⷬ҇ро́кѡвъ.

И҆ взе́мъ части́цꙋ, полага́етъ ю҆ до́лѣ пе́рвыѧ бл҃гочи́ннѡ.

Та́же па́ки глаго́летъ:

Ст҃ы́хъ сла́вныхъ и҆ всехва́льныхъ а҆п҃лъ петра̀ и҆ па́ѵла, и҆ про́чихъ всѣ́хъ ст҃ы́хъ а҆п҃лѡвъ.

И҆ та́кѡ полага́етъ тре́тїю части́цꙋ до́лѣ вторы́ѧ, сконча́вⷬ҇ѧ пе́рвый чи́нъ.

Та́же глаго́летъ:

И҆же во ст҃ы́хъ ѻ҆те́цъ на́шихъ, ст҃и́телей: васі́лїа вели́кагѡ, григо́рїа бг҃осло́ва и҆ і҆ѡа́нна златоꙋ́стагѡ: а҆ѳана́сїа и҆ кѷрі́лла а҆леѯандрі́йскихъ, нїкола́а мѵрлꙋкі́йскагѡ, мїха́йла кі́евскагѡ, петра̀, а҆леѯі́а, і҆ѡ́ны,

Then he says:

Of the holy glorious prophets: Moses and Aaron, Elias and Elisseus, David and Jesse; of the Three holy Youths, of Daniel the Prophet, and of all the holy prophets.

And taking out a particle, he places it below the first, in the proper order.

Then he says again:

Of the holy glorious and all-praised Apostles Peter and Paul, and of all the other holy apostles.

And thus he places the third particle below the second, completing the first row.

Then he says:

Of our fathers among the saints, the holy hierarchs: Basil the Great, Gregory the Theologian, and John Chrysostom; Athanasius and Cyril of Alexandria; Nicholas of Myra in Lycia; Michael of Kiev; Peter, Alexis, Jonah,

філі́ппа, є҆рмоге́на и҆ ты́хѡна, моско́вскихъ, ні́ки́ты новгоро́дскагѡ, леѡнті́а росто́вскагѡ, и҆ всѣ́хъ ст҃ы́хъ ст҃и́телей.

И҆ взе́мъ четве́ртꙋю ча́стицꙋ, полага́етъ ю҆ бли́зъ пе́рвыѧ ча́стицы, творѧ̀ второ́е нача́ло.

Та́же па́ки глаго́летъ:

Ст҃а́гѡ а҆п҃ла, первомч҃нка и҆ а҆рхїдїа́кона стефа́на, ст҃ы́хъ вели́кихъ мч҃нкѡвъ димитрі́а, геѡргі́а, ѳео́дѡра тѵ́рѡна, ѳео́дѡра стратила́та, и҆ всѣ́хъ ст҃ы́хъ мч҃нкъ, и҆ мч҃нцъ: ѳе́клы, варва́ры, кѵрїакі́н, є҆ѵѳиі́мїн и҆ параске́ѵы, є҆катері́ны, и҆ всѣ́хъ ст҃ы́хъ мч҃нцъ.

И҆ взе́мъ пѧ́тꙋю ча́стицꙋ, полага́етъ ю҆ до́лѣ пе́рвыѧ, є҆́ѵцїѧ нача́ломъ втора́гѡ чи́на.

Та́же глаго́летъ:

Прпⷣбныхъ и҆ бг҃оно́сныхъ ѻ҆те́цъ на́шихъ: а҆нтѡ́нїа, є҆ѵⷣꙋ́мїа, са́ввы, ѻ҆нꙋ́фрїа,

Philip, Hermogenes, and Tikhon of Moscow; Nicetas of Novgorod; Leontius of Rostov; and of all the holy hierarchs.

And taking a fourth particle, he places it near the first particle, making the beginning of the second row.

Then again he says:

Of the holy Apostle, Protomartyr, and Archdeacon Stephen; the holy Great martyrs Demetrius, George, Theodore Tyro, Theodore Stratelates, and of all holy martyrs; and of the women martyrs: Thecla, Barbara, Kyriake, Euphemia, and Paraskeve, Catherine, and of all the holy women martyrs.

And taking a fifth particle, he places it below the first which is at the beginning of the second row.

Then he says:

Of our venerable and God-bearing fathers: Anthony, Euthymius, Sabbas, Onuphrius,

а҆ѳана́сїа а҆ѳѡ́нскагѡ, а҆нтѡ́нїа и҆ ѳео́досїа пече́рскихъ, се́ргїа ра́донежскагѡ, варлаа́ма хꙋ́тынскагѡ, серафі́ма саро́вскагѡ, и҆ всѣ́хъ прпⷣбныхъ ѻ҆тє́цъ, и҆ прпⷣбныхъ ма́терей: пелагі́н, ѳео́досїн, а҆настасі́н, є҆ѵпраѯі́н, феврѡ́нїн, ѳеодꙋ́лїн, є҆ѵфроси́нїн, марі́н є҆гѵ́птѧныни, и҆ всѣ́хъ ст҃ы́хъ прпⷣбныхъ ма́терей.

И҆ та́кѡ взе́мъ шестꙋ́ю ча́стицꙋ, полага́етъ ю҆ до́лѣ вторы́ѧ ча́стицы, во и҆сполне́нїе втора́гѡ чи́на.

По си́хъ же глаго́летъ:

Ст҃ы́хъ и҆ чꙋдотво́рцевъ, безсре́бренникъ космы̀ и҆ дамїа́на, кѵ́ра и҆ і҆ѡа́нна, пантелеи́мѡна и҆ є҆рмола́а, и҆ всѣ́хъ ст҃ы́хъ безсре́бренникѡвъ.

И҆ взе́мъ седмꙋ́ю ча́стицꙋ, полага́етъ ю҆ верхꙋ̀, творѧ̀ тре́тїе нача́ло, по чи́нꙋ.

Та́же па́ки глаго́летъ:

Athanasius of Athos, Anthony and Theodosius of the Caves, Sergius of Radonezh, Barlaam of Khutyn, Seraphim of Sarov, and of all the venerable fathers; and of the venerable mothers: Pelagia, Theodosia, Anastasia, Eupraxia, Febronia, Theodulia, Euphrosyne, Mary of Egypt, and of all the venerable mothers.

And taking out a sixth particle, he places it below the second particle, in completion of the second row.

Then he says:

Of the saints and wonderworkers, the Unmercenaries: Cosmas and Damian, Cyrus and John, Panteleimon and Hermolaus, and of all the holy unmercenaries.

And taking out a seventh particle he places it at the top, making the beginning of the third row.

Then again he says:

Ст҃ыхъ и прв҃ныхъ бг҃оотє́цъ іѡакíма и а́нны: и ст҃агѡ и́мк҃ъ [є҆гѡ́же є҆́сть храмъ и є҆гѡ́же є҆́сть де́нь:] ст҃ыхъ равноап҃льныхъ меѳо́дїа и кѷрі́лла, оу҆чи́телей слове́нскихъ: ст҃агѡ равноап҃льнагѡ вели́кагѡ кна́ѕа влади́мїра, и҆ всѣ́хъ ст҃ыхъ, и́хже моли́твами посѣти́ ны, бж҃е.

Й полага́етъ ѻ҆см҃ꙋю части́цꙋ до́лѣ пе́рвыꙗ бл҃гочи́ннѡ.

Є҆ще́ же къ си́мъ глаго́летъ:

Й҆же во ст҃ы́хъ ѻ҆тца̀ на́шегѡ іѡа́нна, а҆рхїеп҃кпа кѡнстантїнопо́льскагѡ, златоꙋ́стагѡ.

А҆́ще пое́тсѧ лїтꙋргі́а є҆гѡ̀, а҆́ще же пое́тсѧ вели́кагѡ васі́лїа, того̀ помина́етъ.

Й та́кѡ взе́мъ девѧ́тꙋю части́цꙋ, полага́етъ ю̀ въ коне́цъ тре́тїагѡ чи́на, во и҆сполне́нїе.

Та́же прїе́мъ четве́ртꙋю просфорꙋ̀, глаго́летъ:

Of the holy and Righteous Ancestors of God, Joachim and Anna; and of Saint(s) N. (whose temple it is and whose day it is); of the holy Equals to the Apostles Methodius and Cyril, teachers of the Slavs; of the holy Equal to the Apostles Great Prince Vladimir, and of all the saints, through whose intercessions do Thou visit us, O God.

And he places the eighth particle below the first, in the proper order.

After this he says:

Of our father among the saints, John Chrysostom, Archbishop of Constantinople.

If his liturgy is sung; but if that of Basil the Great is sung, St Basil is commemorated instead.

And then taking out a ninth particle, he places it at the end of the third row, completing it.

Then taking a fourth prosphora, he says:

Помѧни́, влⷣко чл҃вѣколю́бче, вели́каго господи́на и ѻ҆тца̀ на́шегѡ ст҃ѣ́йшагѡ патрїа́рха и҆м҃къ, и҆ господи́на на́шегѡ высоко_ пресщ҃е́ннѣйшагѡ митрополі́та и҆м҃къ, первоїера́рха р҆у́сскїѧ зару́бѣжныѧ цр҃кве, и҆ господи́на на́шегѡ высокопресщ҃е́ннѣй_ шагѡ а҆рхїепⷭ҇кпа [и҆лѝ пресщ҃е́ннѣйшагѡ є҆пⷭ҇кпа] и҆м҃къ [є҆гѡ́же є҆па́рхїа], честно́е пресвꙋ́терство, во хрⷭ҇тѣ̀ дїа́конство и҆ ве́сь сщ҃е́нническїй чи́нъ, [а҆́ще во ѻ҆би́тели: а҆рхїмандрі́та и҆лѝ и҆гꙋ́мена и҆м҃къ:], и҆ всю̀ бра́тїю на́шꙋ, ꙗ҆́же призва́лъ є҆сѝ во твоѐ ѻ҆бще́нїе, твои́мъ блг҃оꙋ́тробїемъ, всеблг҃і́й влⷣко.

И҆ взе́мъ ча́стицꙋ, полага́етъ ю҆ до́лѣ ст҃а́гѡ хлѣ́ба.

Та́же помина́етъ и҆́же во вла́сти сꙋ́ть, глаго́лѧ си́це:

Помѧни́, гдⷭ҇и, бг҃охрани́мꙋю странꙋ̀ ршссі́йскꙋю и҆ правосла́вныѧ лю́ди є҆ѧ̀ во

Remember, O Master, Lover of Mankind, our great lord and father, the Most Holy Patriarch N., and our lord, the Very Most Reverend Metropolitan N., First Hierarch of the Russian Church Abroad; and our lord the Most [or Right] Reverend Archbishop [or Bishop] N. (whose diocese it is); the honorable priesthood, the diaconate in Christ and all the priestly order, (if in a monastery: Archimandrite or Abbot N.), and all our brethren whom, in Thy compassion, Thou hast called into Thy communion, O All-good Master.

And taking out a particle, he places it below the holy bread.

Then he commemorates those who are in authority, saying thus:

Remember, O Lord, the God-preserved Russian land, and its Orthodox people in the homeland and in the diaspora, this land,

Ѻте́чествїи и въ разсѣ́ѧнїи сꙋ́щїѧ, странꙋ̀ сїю̀, вла́сти и во́инство є҆а̀ и всѣ́хъ вѣ́рою и бл҃гоче́стїемъ живꙋ́щихъ въ не́й.

Та́же помина́етъ, и҆̀хже и҆́мать живы́хъ, по и҆́мени и на ко́еждо и҆́мѧ взе́млетъ ча́стицꙋ, глаго́лѧ:

Помѧнѝ, гдⷭ҇и, и҆҆́мⷬ҇къ:

И҆ та́кѡ взе́мъ ча́стицы, полага́етъ ѧ҆̀ до́лѣ ст҃а́гѡ хлѣ́ба.

Та́же взе́мъ пѧ́тꙋю просфорꙋ̀, глаго́летъ:

Ѽ па́мѧти и ѡ҆ставле́нїи грѣхѡ́въ ст҃ѣ́йшихъ патрїа́рхѡвъ правосла́вныхъ и бл҃гочести́выхъ царе́й и бл҃гочести́выхъ цари́цъ, бл҃же́нныхъ созда́телей ст҃а́гѡ хра́ма сегѡ̀ [а҆́ще во ѻ҆би́тели: ст҃ы́ѧ ѻ҆би́тели сеѧ̀].

Та́же помина́етъ рꙋкоположи́вшаго є҆го̀ а҆рхїере́а и дрꙋги́хъ, и҆́хже хо́щетъ, ᲂу҆со́пшихъ по и҆́мени. На ко́еждо и҆́мѧ взима́етъ ча́стицꙋ, приглаго́лѧ:

its authorities and the armed forces, and all who in faith and piety dwell therein.

Then he commemorates those that are living, by name, and at each name he takes out a particle, saying:

Remember, O Lord, N.

And having taken out a particle, he places it below the holy bread.

Then taking a fifth prosphora, he says:

In commemoration and for the remission of sins of the most holy Orthodox patriarchs, of pious kings and pious queens; and of the blessed founders of this holy temple (if it be a monastery: of this holy monastery).

Then he commemorates the departed, by name: the bishop that ordained him (if he is among the departed), and others, whomsoever he wills. At each name he takes out a particle, saying:

Помѧни̑, гдⷭ҇и: и҆̑мкъ.

И҆ коне́чнѣ глаго́летъ си́це:

И҆ всѣ́хъ въ наде́жди воскрⷭ҇нїѧ, жи́зни вѣ́чныѧ и҆ твоегѡ̀ ѡ҆бще́нїѧ оу҆сѡ́пшихъ правосла́вныхъ ѻ҆тє́цъ и҆ бра́тїй на́шихъ, чл҃вѣколю́бче гдⷭ҇и.

И҆ взима́етъ ча́стицꙋ.

По се́мъ глаго́летъ:

Помѧни̑, гдⷭ҇и, и҆ моѐ недосто́инство, и҆ прости́ ми всѧ́кое согрѣше́нїе, во́льное же и҆ нево́льное.

И҆ взима́етъ ча́стицꙋ.

И҆ прїе́мъ гꙋ́бꙋ, собира́етъ на ді́скосъ ча̑стицы до́лѣ ст҃а́гѡ хлѣ́ба, ꙗ҆́коже бы́ти во оу҆тверже́нїи, и не и҆спа́днꙋти чесомꙋ̀.

Та́же дїа́конъ, прїе́мъ кади́льницꙋ и҆ ѳv́мїамъ вложи́въ въ ню̀, глаго́летъ ко сщ҃е́нникꙋ:

Remember, O Lord, N.

And finally he says thus:

And of all our Orthodox fathers and brethren who have departed in the hope of resurrection, life eternal, and communion with Thee, O Lord, Lover of mankind.

And he takes out a particle.

Then he says:

Remember, O Lord, also mine unworthiness, and pardon me every transgression, both voluntary and involuntary.

And he takes out a particle.

And taking the sponge, he gathers the particles together on the diskos below the holy bread, so that they are secure, and none of them fall off.

Then the deacon, taking the censer and having placed incense in it, says to the priest:

Блгослови, владыко, кадило.

И а҆бїе са́мъ глаго́летъ:

Гдꙋ помо́лимсѧ.

И҆ сщённикъ моли́твꙋ кади́ла:

Кади́ло тебѣ̀ прино́симъ хрⷭ҇тѐ бж҃е на́шъ, въ воню̀ блгоꙋха́нїѧ дх҃о́внагѡ, є҆́же прїе́мъ въ пренбⷭ҇ный тво́й же́ртвенникъ, возниспослѝ на́мъ блгода́ть престг҃ѡ твоегѡ̀ дх҃а.

Дїа́конъ: Гдꙋ помо́лимсѧ.

Сщённикъ, покади́въ ѕвѣздицꙋ, полага́етъ верхꙋ̀ стⷢ҇агѡ хлѣ́ба, глаго́лѧ:

И҆ прише́дши ѕвѣзда̀, ста̀ верхꙋ̀, и҆дѣ́же бѣ̀ ѻ҆троча̀.

Дїа́конъ: Гдꙋ помо́лимсѧ.

І҆ере́й, покади́въ пе́рвый покро́вецъ, покрыва́етъ стый хлѣ́бъ съ дїскосомъ, глаго́лѧ:

Bless the incense, master.

And immediately the deacon himself says:

Let us pray to the Lord.

And the priest says the Prayer of the Incense:

Incense do we offer unto Thee, O Christ our God, as an odour of spiritual fragrance; accepting it upon Thy most heavenly altar, do Thou send down upon us the grace of Thy Most Holy Spirit.

Deacon: Let us pray to the Lord.

The priest, having censed the asterisk, places it over the holy bread, saying:

And the star came and stood over where the young Child was.

Deacon: Let us pray to the Lord.

The priest, having censed the first veil, covers the holy bread and the diskos, saying:

Гдⷭ҇ь воцр҃и́са, въ лѣ́потꙋ ѡ҆блече́са: ѡ҆блече́са гдⷭ҇ь въ си́лꙋ, и҆ препоꙗ́сⷵса. И҆́бо ѹ҆тверди́ вселе́ннꙋю, ꙗ҆́же не подви́житса. Гото́въ прⷵто́лъ тво́й ѿто́лѣ, ѿ вѣ́ка ты̀ є҆сѝ. Воздвиго́ша рѣ́ки, гдⷭ҇и, воздвиго́ша рѣ́ки гла́сы своꙗ̀: во́змꙋтъ рѣ́ки сотре́нїа своꙗ̀, ѿ гла́сѡ́въ во́дъ мно́гихъ. Ди́вны высѡ́ты морскі́а, ди́венъ въ высо́кихъ гдⷭ҇ь, свидѣ́нїа твоꙗ̀ ѹ҆вѣ́ришаса ѕѣлѡ̀: до́мꙋ твоемꙋ̀ подоба́етъ ст҃ы́на, гдⷭ҇и, въ долготꙋ̀ дні́й.

Дїа́конъ: Гдⷭ҇ꙋ помо́лимса. Покры́й, влады́ко.

Їере́й же, покади́въ вторы́й покро́вецъ,
покрыва́етъ ст҃ы́й поти́ръ, глаго́ла:

Покры̀ нб҃са̀ доброде́тель твоꙗ̀, хрⷵтѐ, и҆ хвалы̀ твоеꙗ̀ и҆спо́лнь землѧ̀.
Дїа́конъ: Гдⷭ҇ꙋ помо́лимса. Покры́й, влады́ко.

The Lord is King, He is clothed with majesty; the Lord is clothed in strength, and hath girt Himself, for He hath made the whole world so sure, that it shall not be moved. From the beginning is Thy throne prepared; Thou art from everlasting. The rivers are risen, O Lord, the rivers have lift up their voices. The rivers shall stir up their havoc; from the voices of many waters; wonderful are the heights of the sea; wonderful is the Lord on high. Thy testimonies are very sure; holiness becometh Thine house, O Lord, unto length of days.

Deacon: Let us pray to the Lord. Cover, master.

And the priest, having censed the second veil, covereth the holy chalice, saying:

Thy virtue covered the heavens, O Christ, and the earth is full of Thy praise.

Deacon: Let us pray to the Lord. Cover, master.

І҆ере́й же, покади́въ покро́въ,
си́рѣчь возду́хъ, и҆ покрыва́а ѻ҆бо́а,
глаго́летъ:

Покры́й на́съ кро́вомъ крилꙋ̀ твое́ю, и҆
ѿженѝ ѿ на́съ вса́каго врага̀ и҆ сꙋпоста́та:
оу҆мири́ на́шꙋ жи́знь, гдⷵи, помилꙋ́й на́съ,
и҆ мі́ръ тво́й, и҆ спасѝ дꙋ́шы на́ша, а҆́кѡ
бл҃гъ и҆ чл҃вѣколю́бецъ.

Та́же прїе́мъ сщ҃е́нникъ кади́льницꙋ, кади́тъ
предложе́нїе, глаго́ла три́жды:

Бл҃гослове́нъ бг҃ъ на́шъ, си́це бл҃говоли́вый,
сла́ва тебѣ̀.

Дїа́конъ же на ко́емждо глаго́летъ:

Всегда̀, ны́нѣ и҆ при́снѡ, и҆ во вѣ́ки вѣкѡ́въ.
А҆ми́нь.

И҆ покланѧ́ютса бл҃гоговѣ́йнѡ ѻ҆́ба,
три́жды.

Та́же прїе́мъ дїа́конъ кади́льницꙋ, глаго́летъ:

Then the priest, having censed the veil, i.e. the aer, covers both the holy diskos and the holy chalice, saying:

Shelter us with the shelter of Thy wings, and drive away from us every enemy and adversary. Make our life peaceful, O Lord, have mercy on us, and on Thy world, and save our souls, for Thou art good and the Lover of mankind.

Then, taking the censer, the priest censes the offering, saying thrice:

Blessed is our God Who is thus well pleased, glory to Thee.

And the deacon says each time:

Always, now and ever, and unto the ages of ages. Amen.

And both bow reverently, thrice.

Then, taking the censer, the deacon says:

Ѿ предложе́нныхъ че́тныхъ дарѣ́хъ, гдꙋ помо́лимсѧ.

Сщ҃е́нникъ же мл҃твꙋ предложе́нїѧ:

Бж҃е, бж҃е на́шъ, нбⷭ҇ный хлѣ́бъ, пи́щꙋ всемꙋ̀ мі́рꙋ, гдⷭ҇а на́шего и҆ бг҃а і҆и҃са хрⷭ҇та̀ посла́вый сп҃са, и҆ и҆зба́вителѧ и҆ бл҃годѣ́телѧ, блⷭ҇вѧ́ща и҆ ѡ҆сщ҃а́юща на́съ, са́мъ блⷭ҇вѝ предложе́нїе сїѐ, и҆ прїимѝ є҆̀ въ пренбⷭ҇ный тво́й же́ртвенникъ. Помѧнѝ, ꙗ҆́кѡ бл҃гъ и҆ чл҃вѣколю́бецъ, принесшихъ, и҆ и҆́хже ра́ди принесо́ша: и҆ на́съ неѡсꙋжде́ны сохранѝ во сщ҃еннодѣ́йствїи бжⷭ҇твенныхъ твои́хъ та́инъ. Ꙗ҆́кѡ ст҃и́сѧ и҆ просла́висѧ пречⷭ҇тно́е, и҆ великолѣ́пое и҆́мѧ тво́е, ѻ҆ц҃а̀, и҆ сн҃а, и҆ ст҃а́гѡ дх҃а, ны́нѣ и҆ при́снѡ, и҆ во вѣ́ки вѣкѡ́въ. А҆ми́нь.

И҆ посе́мъ твори́тъ ѿпꙋ́стъ та́мѡ, глаго́лѧ си́це:

For the precious gifts set forth, let us pray to the Lord.

And the priest says the Prayer of Oblation:

O God, our God, Who didst send forth the Heavenly Bread, the food of the whole world, our Lord and God, Jesus Christ, the Saviour and Redeemer and Benefactor Who blesseth and sanctifieth us: Do Thou Thyself bless this offering, and accept it upon Thine altar above the heavens. As Thou art good and the Lover of mankind, remember those that offer it, and those for whose sake it was offered; and keep us uncondemned in the ministry of Thy Divine Mysteries. For hallowed and glorified is Thy most honorable and majestic name: of the Father, and of the Son, and of the Holy Spirit, now and ever, and unto the ages of ages. Amen.

And after this he pronounces the dismissal there, saying:

Сла́ва тебѣ̀, хрⷭ҇тѐ бж҃е, оу҆пова́нїе на́ше, сла́ва тебѣ̀.

Дїа́конъ: Сла́ва, и҆ ны́нѣ: Гдⷭ҇и, поми́лꙋй, три́жды. Бл҃гословѝ.

Сщ҃е́нникъ глаго́летъ ѿпꙋ́стъ:

А҆́ще оу҆́бѡ є҆́сть недѣ́ла: Воскрⷭ҇ый и҆з̾ ме́ртвыхъ:

А҆́ще же нѝ: Хрⷭ҇то́съ и҆́стинный бг҃ъ на́шъ, мл҃твами пречⷭ҇тыа своеѧ̀ мт҃ре, и҆́же во ст҃ы́хъ ѻ҆тца̀ на́шегѡ і҆ѡа́нна, а҆рхїепⷭ҇кпа кѡнстантїнопо́льскагѡ, златоꙋ́стагѡ [а҆́ще же соверша́етсѧ лїтꙋргі́а вели́кагѡ васі́лїа, глаго́летъ: васі́лїа вели́кагѡ, а҆рхїепⷭ҇кпа кеса́рїи каппадокі́нскїѧ:] и҆ всѣ́хъ ст҃ы́хъ, поми́лꙋетъ и҆ спасе́тъ на́съ, ꙗ҆́кѡ бл҃гъ и҆ чл҃вѣколю́бецъ.

Дїа́конъ: А҆ми́нь.

По ѿпꙋ́стѣ же кади́тъ дїа́конъ ст҃о́е предложе́нїе. Та́же ѿхо́дитъ, и҆ кади́тъ

Glory to Thee, O Christ God, our hope, glory to Thee.

Deacon: Glory . . . both now . . . Amen. Lord have mercy. Thrice. Bless.

The priest says the dismissal:

If it be Sunday: May Christ our true God, Who rose from the dead, . . .

If not: May Christ our true God, through the intercessions of His most pure Mother; of our father among the saints, John Chrysostom, Archbishop of Constantinople; (If the Liturgy of Basil the Great be celebrated, he says: Basil the Great, Archbishop of Caesarea in Cappadocia;) and of all the saints, have mercy on us and save us, for He is good and the Lover of mankind.

Deacon: Amen.

After the dismissal, the deacon censes the holy offering. Then he goes and censes the

сті́ю трапе́зꙋ крꙋго́мъ крестовидню,
глаго́лѧ въ себѣ̀:

Во гробѣ̀ пло́тски, во а́дѣ же съ дꙋшє́ю
ꙗ́кѡ бг҃ъ, въ раи́ же съ разбо́йникомъ, и̑
на пртⷭ҇о́лѣ бы́лъ ᲄ҇сѝ, хрⷭ҇тѐ, со ѻ̑ц҃е́мъ и̑
дх҃омъ, всѧ̑ и̑сполнѧ́ѧй неѡпи́санный.

Та́же ѱало́мъ н҃-й, Поми́лꙋй мѧ̀, бж҃е:
въ не́мже и̑ покади́въ сти́лище же и̑
хра́мъ ве́сь, вхо́дитъ па́ки во ст҃ы́й
ѻ̑лта́рь, и̑ покади́въ сті́ю трапе́зꙋ па́ки,
и̑ сщ҃е́нника, кади́льницꙋ ᲂу̑́бѡ ѿлага́етъ
на мѣ́сто своѐ, са́мъ же прихо́дитъ ко
і̑ере́ю. И̑ ста́вше вкꙋ́пѣ пре́д сті́ю
трапе́зою, покланѧ́ютсѧ три́жды,
въ себѣ̀ молѧ́щесѧ, и̑ глаго́люще:

Цр҃ю̀ нбⷭ҇ный, ᲂу̑тѣ́шителю, дш҃е и̑́стины,
и́же вездѣ̀ сы́й, и̑ всѧ̑ и̑сполнѧ́ѧй,
сокро́вище бл҃ги́хъ и̑ жи́зни пода́телю:

Holy Table round about in the shape of a
cross, saying silently:

In the grave bodily, but in Hades with Thy
soul as God; in Paradise with the thief, and
on the throne with the Father and the Spirit
wast Thou Who fillest all things, O Christ
the Inexpressible.

Then the 50th Psalm: Have mercy on me,
O God . . . during which, having censed
the sanctuary and the whole temple, he
enters again into the holy altar, and having
again censed the Holy Table, and the priest,
he puts aside the censer into its place,
and approaches the priest. And standing
together before the Holy Table, they bow
down thrice, while praying secretly, saying:

O Heavenly King, Comforter, Spirit of
Truth, Who art everwhere present and fillest
all things, Treasury of good things and Giver
of life: Come and dwell in us, and cleanse us

пріиди̂ и̂ всели́са въ ны̀, и̂ ѡ҆чи́сти ны̀ ѿ
вса́кіа скве́рны, и̂ спси̂, бл҃же, дꙋ́шы на́ша.

Сла́ва въ вы́шнихъ бг҃ꙋ, и̂ на земли̂
мі́ръ, въ чл҃вѣ́цѣхъ бл҃говоле́ніе. в҃-жды.

Гд҃и, ᲂу҆стнѣ̀ мои̂ ѿве́рзеши, и̂ ᲂу҆ста̀
моа̀ возвѣста́тъ хвалꙋ̀ твою̀.

Та́же цѣлꙋ́ютъ, сщ҃е́нникъ ᲂу҆́бѡ ст҃о́е е҆ѵⷢ҇лїе,
діа́конъ же ст҃ꙋ́ю трапе́зꙋ.

И̂ посе́мъ подкло́нивъ діа́конъ свою̀ главꙋ̀
сщ҃е́нникꙋ, держа̀ и̂ ѻ҆ра́рь треми̂ пе́рсты
десны́а рꙋки̂, глаго́летъ:

Вре́ма сотвори́ти гд҃ви, влады́ко, бл҃гослови̂.

Сщ҃е́нникъ, зна́менꙋа е҆го̀, глаго́летъ:

Бл҃гослове́нъ бг҃ъ на́шъ всегда̀, ны́нѣ и̂
при́снѡ, и̂ во вѣ́ки вѣкѡ́въ.

Та́же діа́конъ: Помоли́са ѡ҆ мнѣ̀, влады́ко
ст҃ы́й.

Сщ҃е́нникъ: Да и̂спра́витъ гд҃ь стѡпы̀ твоа̂.

of all impurity, and save our souls, O Good One.

Glory to God in the highest, and on earth peace, good will among men. Twice.

O Lord, open Thou my lips, and my mouth shall show forth Thy praise.

Then the priest kisses the Holy Gospel, and the deacon the Holy Table.

After this, the deacon, bowing his head to the priest, and holding his orarion with three fingers of his right hand, says:

It is time for the Lord to act. Master, bless.

The priest, signing him with the sign of the Cross, says:

Blessed is our God, always, now and ever, and unto the ages of ages.

Then the deacon: Pray for me, holy master.

Priest: May the Lord direct thy steps.

И҆ па́ки дїа́конъ: Помѧни́ мѧ, влады́ко
ст҃ый.

Сщ҃е́нникъ: Да помѧне́тъ тѧ̀ гдⷭ҇ь бг҃ъ во
црⷭ҇твїи свое́мъ, всегда̀, ны́нѣ и҆ при́снѡ, и҆
во вѣ́ки вѣкѡ́въ.

Дїа́конъ же: А҆ми́нь.

И҆ поклони́всѧ, и҆схо́дитъ сѣ́верными
две́рьми, поне́же црⷭ҇кїѧ две́ри до вхо́да
не ѿверза́ютсѧ. И҆ ста́въ на ѻ҆бы́чнѣмъ
мѣ́стѣ, прѧ́мѡ ст҃ы́хъ двере́й,
поклонѧ́етсѧ со бл҃гоговѣ́нїемъ,
три́жды, глаго́лѧ въ себѣ̀:

Гдⷭ҇и, ѹ҆стнѣ̀ мои̑ ѿве́рзеши, и҆ ѹ҆ста̀ моѧ̑
возвѣстѧ́тъ хвалꙋ̀ твою̀.

И҆ посе́мъ начина́етъ глаго́лати:

Бл҃гословѝ, влады́ко.

И҆ начина́етъ сщ҃е́нникъ:

Бл҃гослове́но црⷭ҇тво:

And again the deacon: **Remember me, holy master.**

Priest: **May the Lord God remember thee in His kingdom, always, now and ever, and unto the ages of ages.**

Deacon: **Amen.**

And having bowed, he goes out by the north door, because the royal doors are not opened until the entrance. And standing in the usual place, directly before the holy doors, he bows reverently thrice, saying secretly:

O Lord, open Thou my lips, and my mouth shall show forth Thy praise.

And afterwards he begins, saying:

Bless, master.

And the priest begins:

Blessed is the kingdom . . .

Вѣдати подобаетъ: а́ще безъ дїа́кона слꙋ́житъ їере́й, въ проскомі́дїи дїа́конскихъ сло́въ, и̑ на лїтꙋ́ргі́и пред̾ є҆ѵⷢлїемъ, и̑ на ѿвѣ́тъ є҆гѡ̀: Блⷢгослови̑, влады́ко, и̑ Проводи̑, влады́ко, и̑ Вре́мѧ сотвори́ти, да не глаго́летъ, то́чїю є҆ктенї́й и̑ чино́вное предложе́нїе.

А҆́ще же собо́ромъ слꙋ́жатъ сщ҃е́ннїи мно́зи, дѣ́йство проскомі́дїи є҆ди́нъ їере́й то́кмѡ да твори́тъ, и̑ глаго́летъ и̑з̾ѡбраже́ннаѧ. Про́чїи же слꙋжи́телє ничто́же проскомі́дїи ѻ҆со́бнѡ да глаго́лютъ.

It is important to note that if a priest serves without a deacon, the words of the deacon in the Proskomedia, and during the Liturgy before the Gospel, and his response: **Bless, master,** and **Pierce, master,** and **It is time to act,** . . . are not said, but only the litanies and the rite of the Proskomedia.

If many priests concelebrate, the rite of the Proskomedia is celebrated by only one priest who says what is set forth. None of the other celebrants, however, shall say anything of the Proskomedia themselves.

Бжⷭ҇твеннаѧ Лїтꙋргі́а

Дїа́конъ: Блⷭ҇гословѝ, влады́ко.

Їере́й:

Бл҃гослове́но црⷭ҇тво ѻ҆ц҃а̀, и҆ сн҃а, и҆ ст҃а́гѡ дх҃а, ны́нѣ и҆ при́снѡ, и҆ во вѣ́ки вѣкѡ́въ.

Ли́къ: А҆ми́нь.

Дїа́конъ: Ми́ромъ гдⷭ҇ꙋ помо́лимсѧ.

Ли́къ: Гдⷭ҇и, поми́лꙋй.

Дїа́конъ: Ѡ҆ свы́шнѣмъ ми́рѣ, и҆ спасе́нїи дꙋ́шъ на́шихъ, гдⷭ҇ꙋ помо́лимсѧ.

Ли́къ: Гдⷭ҇и, поми́лꙋй.

Дїа́конъ: Ѡ҆ ми́рѣ всегѡ̀ мі́ра, бл҃гостоѧ́нїи ст҃ы́хъ бж҃їихъ цр҃кве́й, и҆ соедине́нїи всѣ́хъ, гдⷭ҇ꙋ помо́лимсѧ.

Ли́къ: Гдⷭ҇и, поми́лꙋй.

The Divine Liturgy

Deacon: Bless, master.

Priest:

Blessed is the kingdom of the Father, and of the Son, and of the Holy Spirit, now and ever, and unto the ages of ages.

Choir: Amen.

Deacon: In peace let us pray to the Lord.

Choir: Lord, have mercy.

Deacon: For the peace from above, and the salvation of our souls, let us pray to the Lord.

Choir: Lord, have mercy.

Deacon: For the peace of the whole world, the good estate of the holy churches of God, and the union of all, let us pray to the Lord.

Choir: Lord, have mercy.

Дїа́конъ: Ѡ҆ ст҃ѣ́мъ хра́мѣ се́мъ, и҆ съ вѣ́рою, бл҃гоговѣ́нїемъ и҆ стра́хомъ бж҃їимъ входѧ́щихъ во́нь, гдꙋ̀ помо́лимсѧ.

Ли́къ: Гдⷭ҇и, поми́лꙋй.

Дїа́конъ: Ѡ҆ вели́комъ господи́нѣ и҆ ѻ҆тцѣ̀ на́шемъ ст҃ѣ́йшемъ патрїа́рсѣ и҆́мⷬ҇къ, и҆ ѡ҆ господи́нѣ на́шемъ высокопреѡсщ҃е́н_ нѣ́йшемъ митрополі́тѣ и҆́мⷬ҇къ, первоїера́рсѣ рꙋ́сскїѧ зарꙋбе́жныѧ цр҃кве, и҆ ѡ҆ господи́нѣ на́шемъ высокопреѡсщ҃е́ннѣйшемъ а҆рхїе_ пⷭ҇кпѣ [и҆лѝ преѡсщ҃е́ннѣйшемъ є҆пⷭ҇кпѣ] и҆́мⷬ҇къ, честнѣ́мъ пресвѵ́терствѣ, во хрⷭ҇тѣ̀ дїа́констѣ, ѡ҆ все́мъ при́чтѣ и҆ лю́дехъ, гдꙋ̀ помо́лимсѧ.

Ли́къ: Гдⷭ҇и, поми́лꙋй.

Дїа́конъ: Ѡ҆ странѣ̀ се́й, власте́хъ и҆ во́инствѣ є҆ѧ̀, и҆ всѣ́хъ вѣ́рою и҆ бл҃гоче́стїемъ живꙋ́щихъ въ не́й, гдꙋ̀ помо́лимсѧ.

Ли́къ: Гдⷭ҇и, поми́лꙋй.

Дїа́конъ: Ѡ҆ бг҃охрани́мѣй странѣ̀ рѡссі́йстѣй и҆ правосла́вныхъ лю́дехъ є҆ѧ̀ во ѻ҆те́чествїи и҆ разсѣ́ѧнїи сꙋ́щихъ и҆ ѡ҆ спⷭ҇е́нїи и҆́хъ, гдꙋ̀ помо́лимсѧ.

Deacon: For this holy temple, and for them that with faith, reverence, and the fear of God enter herein, let us pray to the Lord.

Choir: Lord, have mercy.

Deacon: For our great lord and father, the Most Holy Patriarch N.; for our lord, the Very Most Reverend Metropolitan N., First Hierarch of the Russian Church Abroad; for our lord, the Most [or Right] Reverend Archbishop [or Bishop] N.; for the honorable priesthood, the diaconate in Christ, for all the clergy and people, let us pray to the Lord.

Choir: Lord, have mercy.

Deacon: For this land, its authorities and armed forces, and all who with faith and piety dwell therein, let us pray to the Lord.

Choir: Lord, have mercy.

Deacon: For the God-preserved Russian land and its Orthodox people both in the homeland and in the diaspora, and for their salvation, let us pray to the Lord.

Ли́къ: Гди, поми́луй.

Діа́конъ: Ѽ є́же изба́вити лю́ди своѧ̀ ѿ вра̑гъ ви́димыхъ и неви́димыхъ, въ на́съ же оу҆тверди́ти є҆диномы́сліе, братолю́біе и бл҃гоче́стїе, гдѹ помо́лимсѧ.

Ли́къ: Гди, поми́луй.

Діа́конъ: Ѽ гра́дѣ се́мъ [и҆лѝ ѽ ве́си се́й, и҆лѝ ѽ ст҃ѣй ѻ҆би́тели се́й], всѧ́комъ гра́дѣ, странѣ̀, и вѣ́рою живу́щихъ въ ни́хъ, гдѹпомо́лимсѧ.

Ли́къ: Гди, поми́луй.

Діа́конъ: Ѽ бл҃горастворе́нїи воздѹ́ховъ, ѽ и҆з ѻ҆би́лїи плодѡ́въ земны́хъ, и време́нѣхъ ми́рныхъ, гдѹ помо́лимсѧ.

Ли́къ: Гди, поми́луй.

Діа́конъ: Ѽ пла́вающихъ, пѹтеше́ст_вѹющихъ, недѹ́гѹющихъ, стра́ждѹщихъ, плѣне́нныхъ, и ѽ спасе́нїи и́хъ, гдѹ помо́лимсѧ.

Ли́къ: Гди, поми́луй.

Діа́конъ: Ѽ и҆зба́витисѧ на́мъ ѿ всѧ́кїѧ ско́рби, гнѣ́ва и нѹ́жды, гдѹ помо́лимсѧ.

Choir: Lord, have mercy.

Deacon: That He may deliver His people from enemies visible and invisible, and confirm in us oneness of mind, brotherly love, and piety, let us pray to the Lord.

Choir: Lord, have mercy.

Deacon: For this city [or village, or holy monastery], for every city and country, and the faithful that dwell therein, let us pray to the Lord.

Choir: Lord, have mercy.

Deacon: For seasonable weather, abundance of the fruits of the earth, and peaceful times, let us pray to the Lord.

Choir: Lord, have mercy.

Deacon: For travelers by sea, land and air, for the sick, the suffering, the captives, and for their salvation, let us pray to the Lord.

Choir: Lord, have mercy.

Deacon: That we may be delivered from all tribulation, wrath, and necessity, let us pray to the Lord.

Ли́къ: Гдⷭи, поми́луй.

Дїа́конъ: Засту́пи, спаси́, поми́луй, и
сохрани́ на́съ, бже, твое́ю блгⷣа́тїю.

Ли́къ: Гдⷭи, поми́луй.

Дїа́конъ: Прест҃у́ю, пречтⷭу́ю, преблго_
слове́нную, сла́вную влⷣчцу на́шу бцⷣу
и приснодв҃у мрі́ю со все́ми ст҃ы́ми
помяну́вше, са́ми себе́, и дру́гъ дру́га, и
ве́сь живо́тъ на́шъ хрⷭту́ бг҃у предади́мъ.

Ли́къ: Тебѣ̀, гдⷭи.

Моли́тва пе́рвагѡ антїфѡ́на та́йнѡ
глаго́летсѧ ѿ їере́а:

Гдⷭи бже на́шъ, є҆гѡ́же держа́ва
несказа́нна, и сла́ва непостижи́ма,
є҆гѡ́же млⷭть безмѣ́рна и чл҃вѣколю́бїе
неизрече́нно: са́мъ, влⷣко, по блгоутро́бїю
твоему̀, при́зри на ны̀ и на ст҃ы́й хра́мъ
се́й, и сотвори́ съ на́ми, и молѧ́щимисѧ
съ на́ми, бога́тыя ми́лѡсти твоѧ̑ и
щедрѡ́ты твоѧ̑.

Choir: Lord, have mercy.

Deacon: Help us, save us, have mercy on us, and keep us, O God, by Thy grace.

Choir: Lord, have mercy.

Deacon: Calling to remembrance our most holy, most pure, most blessed, glorious Lady Theotokos and Ever-Virgin Mary with all the saints, let us commit ourselves and one another and all our life unto Christ, our God.

Choir: To Thee, O Lord.

The priest secretly says the prayer of the first antiphon:

O Lord our God, Whose dominion is indescribable, and Whose glory is incomprehensible, Whose mercy is infinite, and Whose love for mankind is ineffable: Do Thou Thyself, O Master, according to Thy tender compassion, look upon us, and upon this holy temple, and deal with us, and them that pray with us, according to Thine abundant mercies and compassion.

Возглаше́нїе: Ꙗ҆́кѡ подоба́етъ тебѣ̀ всѧ́каѧ сла́ва, че́сть и҆ поклоне́нїе, ѻ҆ц҃ꙋ, и҆ сн҃ꙋ, и҆ ст҃о́мꙋ дх҃ꙋ, ны́нѣ и҆ при́снѡ, и҆ во вѣ́ки вѣкѡ́въ.

Ли́къ: А҆ми́нь.

Дїа́конъ поклони́всѧ ᲂу҆стꙋпа́етъ ѿ мѣ́ста своегѡ̀, и҆ ѿше́дъ стои́тъ пред̾ і҆кѡ́ною хрⷭ҇то́вою, держа̀ и҆ ѻ҆ра́рь треми́ пе́рсты десны́ѧ рꙋ́ки.

И҆ пое́тсѧ пе́рвый а҆нтїфѡ́нъ ѿ пѣвцє́въ:

Бл҃гословѝ, дꙋшѐ моѧ̀, гдⷭ҇а, бл҃гослове́нъ є҆сѝ гдⷭ҇и. Бл҃гословѝ, дꙋшѐ моѧ̀, гдⷭ҇а, и҆ всѧ̑ внꙋ́треннѧѧ моѧ̑, и҆́мѧ ст҃о́е є҆гѡ̀. Бл҃гословѝ, дꙋшѐ моѧ̀, гдⷭ҇а, и҆ не забыва́й всѣ́хъ воздаѧ́нїй є҆гѡ̀: ѡ҆чища́ющаго всѧ̑ беззакѡ́нїѧ твоѧ̑, и҆сцѣлѧ́ющаго всѧ̑ недꙋ́ги твоѧ̑: и҆збавлѧ́ющаго ѿ и҆стлѣ́нїѧ живо́тъ твой, вѣнча́ющаго тѧ̀ ми́лостїю и҆ щедро́тами: и҆сполнѧ́ющаго во бл҃ги́хъ жела́нїе твоѐ: ѡ҆бнови́тсѧ ꙗ҆́кѡ ѻ҆рла̀ ю҆́ность твоѧ̀. Творѧ́й ми́лостыни гдⷭ҇ь, и҆ сꙋдьбꙋ̀ всѣ̑мъ ѡ҆би́димымъ. Сказа̀ пꙋти̑ своѧ̑ мѡѷсе́ови, сыновѡ́мъ і҆и҃левымъ хотѣ́нїѧ

Exclamation: For unto Thee is due all glory, honor and worship, to the Father, and to the Son, and to the Holy Spirit, now and ever, and unto the ages of ages.

Choir: Amen.

The deacon, bowing, steps aside from his place and stands before the icon of Christ, holding his orarion with three fingers of his right hand.

And the first antiphon is sung by the choir:

Bless the Lord, O my soul; blessed art Thou, O Lord. Bless the Lord, O my soul, and all that is within me bless His holy Name. Bless the Lord, O my soul, and forget not all His benefits; Who forgiveth all thine iniquities, and healeth all thy diseases; Who redeemeth thy life from corruption, and crowneth thee with mercy and compassion; Who satisfieth thy desire with good things; thy youth shall be renewed like the eagle's. The Lord performeth deeds of mercy, and judgment for all them that are wronged. He made known His

своⷶ. Щедⷬ҇ и млⷭ҇тивъ гдⷭ҇ь, долготерпѣливъ и многомлⷭ҇тивъ.

Блⷢ҇гослови, душе моѧ, гдⷭ҇а, и всѧ внутреннѧѧ моѧ, имѧ стⷪ҇е єгⷰ҇.

Блⷢ҇гословенъ єси, гдⷭ҇и.

По исполненіи же антіфѡна, пришедъ діаконъ и ставъ на ѻбычнемъ мѣстѣ и поклонивсѧ, глаголетъ:

Паки и паки миромъ гдⷭ҇у помолимсѧ.

Ликъ: Гдⷭ҇и, помилуй.

Діаконъ: Заступи, спаси, помилуй и сохрани насъ, бже, твоею блⷢ҇годатію.

Ликъ: Гдⷭ҇и, помилуй.

Діаконъ: Престⷭ҇ую, пречтⷭ҇ую, пребл҇гословенную, славную влⷣчцу нашу бцⷣу и приснодѣву мрⷪ҇ію со всⷪ҇ѣми стⷭ҇ыми помѧнувше, сами себе, и другъ друга, и весь животъ нашъ хрⷭ҇ту бгⷭ҇у предадимъ.

Ликъ: Тебѣ, гдⷭ҇и.

ways unto Moses, His will unto the children of Israel. The Lord is compassionate and merciful, long-suffering, and of great kindness.

Bless the Lord, O my soul, and all that is within me bless His holy Name.

Blessed art Thou, O Lord.

At the conclusion of the antiphon, the deacon, having returned to his usual place and bowed, says:

Again and again, in peace let us pray to the Lord.

Choir: Lord, have mercy.

Deacon: Help us, save us, have mercy on us, and keep us, O God, by Thy grace.

Choir: Lord, have mercy.

Deacon: Calling to remembrance our most holy, most pure, most blessed, glorious Lady Theotokos and Ever-Virgin Mary, with all the saints, let us commit ourselves and one another and all our life unto Christ, our God.

Choir: To Thee, O Lord.

Моли́тва втора́гѡ а҆нтїфѡ́на та́йнѡ
глаго́летсѧ ѿ і҆ере́а:

Г҃ди бж҃е на́шъ, сп҃си лю́ди твоѧ̑ и҆
бл҃гослови̑ достоѧ́нїе твое́, и҆сполне́нїе
цр҃кве твоеѧ̀ сохранѝ, ѡ҆ст҃ѝ лю́бѧщыѧ
бл҃голѣ́пїе до́мꙋ твоегѡ̀: ты̀ тѣ́хъ
возпросла́ви бж҃е́ственною твое́ю си́лою, и҆
не ѡ҆ста́ви на́съ ᲂу҆пова́ющихъ на тѧ̀.
Возглаше́нїе: Ꙗ҆́кѡ твоѧ̀ держа́ва, и҆ твое́
є҆́сть цр҃тво и҆ си́ла и҆ сла́ва, ѻ҆ц҃а̀, и҆ сн҃а,
и҆ ст҃а́гѡ дх҃а, ны́нѣ и҆ при́снѡ, и҆ во вѣ́ки
вѣкѡ́въ.

Ли́къ: А҆ми́нь.

И҆ пое́тсѧ подо́бнѣ ѿ пѣвце́въ вторы́й
а҆нтїфѡ́нъ: дїа́конъ же подо́бнѣ твори́тъ,
ꙗ҆́коже и҆ въ пе́рвой моли́твѣ.

Сла́ва ѻ҆ц҃ꙋ̀, и҆ сн҃ꙋ, и҆ ст҃о́мꙋ дх҃ꙋ.

Хвалѝ, дꙋшѐ моѧ̀, гд҃а. Восхвалю̀ гд҃а въ
живо́тѣ мое́мъ, пою̀ бг҃ꙋ мое́мꙋ, до́ндеже

The priest secretly says the prayer of the second antiphon:

O Lord our God, save Thy people and bless Thine inheritance, preserve the fullness of Thy Church, sanctify them that love the beauty of Thy house; do Thou glorify them by Thy divine power, and forsake not us that hope in Thee.

Exclamation: For Thine is the dominion, and Thine is the kingdom, and the power, and the glory, of the Father, and of the Son, and of the Holy Spirit, now and ever, and unto the ages of ages.

Choir: Amen.

And the second antiphon is sung by the choir in like manner to the first. The deacon does also as during the first prayer.

Glory to the Father, and to the Son, and to the Holy Spirit.

Praise the Lord, O my soul. While I live will I praise the Lord; I will sing unto my God

є҆́смь. Не надѣ́йтесѧ на кнѧ́зи, на сы́ны
человѣ́ческїѧ, въ ни́хже нѣ́сть спⷭ҇нїѧ.
И҆зы́детъ дꙋ́хъ є҆гѡ̀, и҆ возврати́тсѧ въ
зе́млю свою̀: въ то́й де́нь поги́бнꙋтъ всѧ̑
помышлє́нїѧ є҆гѡ̀. Бл҃же́нъ, є҆мꙋ́же бг҃ъ
і҆а́кѡвль помо́щникъ є҆гѡ̀, ᲂу҆пова́нїе є҆гѡ̀ на
гдⷭ҇а бг҃а своегѡ̀: Сотво́ршаго нб҃о и҆ зе́млю, мо́ре,
и҆ всѧ̑, ꙗ҆́же въ ни́хъ: Хранѧ́щаго и҆́стинꙋ въ
вѣ́къ, творѧ́щаго сꙋ́дъ ѡ҆би̑димымъ, даю́щаго
пи́щꙋ а҆́лчꙋщымъ. Гдⷭ҇ь рѣши́тъ ѡ҆кова̑нныѧ,
гдⷭ҇ь ᲂу҆мꙋдрѧ́етъ слѣпцы̀, гдⷭ҇ь возво́дитъ
низве́ржєнныѧ, гдⷭ҇ь лю́битъ пра́ведники. Гдⷭ҇ь
храни́тъ прише́льцы, си́ра и҆ вдовꙋ̀ прїи́метъ, и҆
пꙋ́ть грѣ́шныхъ погꙋби́тъ. Воцр҃и́тсѧ гдⷭ҇ь во
вѣ́къ, бг҃ъ тво́й, сїѡ́не, въ ро́дъ и҆ ро́дъ.

И҆ ны́нѣ и҆ при́снѡ, и҆ во вѣ́ки вѣкѡ́въ.
А҆ми́нь.

Є҆диноро́дный сн҃е, и҆ сло́ве бж҃їй, безсме́ртенъ
сы́й, и҆ и҆зво́ливый спⷭ҇нїѧ на́шегѡ ра́ди
воплоти́тисѧ ѿ ст҃ы́ѧ бцⷣы, и҆ приснодѣ́вы
мр҃і́и, непрело́жнѡ вочл҃вѣ́чивыйсѧ: распны́йсѧ
же хрⷭ҇тѐ бж҃е, сме́ртїю сме́рть попра́вый,

as long as I have being. O put not your trust in princes, in the sons of men, in whom there is no salvation. His spirit shall go forth, and he shall return again to his earth; in that day all his thoughts shall perish. Blessed is he that hath the God of Jacob for his helper, whose hope is in the Lord his God; Who made heaven and earth, the sea, and all that therein is, Who preserveth truth for ever; Who rendereth judgement for the wronged, Who giveth food unto the hungry; The Lord looseth the fettered; the Lord giveth wisdom to the blind; the Lord raiseth up the fallen; the Lord loveth the righteous; the Lord preserveth the proselytes; He defendeth the fatherless and the widow, but the way of sinners shall He destroy. The Lord shall reign forever; thy God, O Sion, unto generation and generation.

Both now, and ever, and unto the ages of ages. Amen.

O Only-begotten Son and Word of God, Who art immortal, yet didst deign for our salvation to become incarnate of the holy Theotokos and Ever-Virgin Mary, and without change didst become man, and wast crucified,

є҆ди́нъ сы́й ст҃ы́ѧ трⷪ҇цы, спрославлѧ́емый ѻ҆ц҃ꙋ
и҆ ст҃о́мꙋ дх҃ꙋ, сп҃си́ на́съ.

Дїа́конъ: Па́ки и҆ па́ки ми́ромъ гдⷭ҇ꙋ помо́-
лимсѧ.

Ли́къ: Гдⷭ҇и, поми́лꙋй.

Дїа́конъ: Застꙋпи́, спаси́, поми́лꙋй и҆
сохрани́ на́съ бж҃е, твое́ю бл҃года́тїю.

Ли́къ: Гдⷭ҇и, поми́лꙋй.

Дїа́конъ: Прест҃ꙋ́ю, пречⷭ҇тꙋ́ю, пребл҃го-
слове́ннꙋю, сла́внꙋю вл҃чцꙋ на́шꙋ бцⷣꙋ
и҆ приснодв҃ꙋ мр҃і́ю со все́ми ст҃ы́ми
помѧнꙋ́вше, са́ми себѐ, и҆ дрꙋ́гъ дрꙋ́га, и҆
ве́сь живо́тъ на́шъ хрⷭ҇тꙋ́ бг҃ꙋ предади́мъ.

Ли́къ: Тебѣ̀, гдⷭ҇и.

Моли́тва тре́тїагѡ а҆нтїфѡ́на та́йнѡ
глаго́летсѧ ѿ і҆ере́а:

И҆́же ѻ҆́бщыѧ сїѧ̑, и҆ согла́сныѧ
дарова́вый на́мъ мл҃твы, и҆́же и҆ двѣма̀
и҆лѝ тре́мъ соглаꙋ́ющымсѧ ѡ҆ и҆́мени
твое́мъ проше́нїѧ пода́ти ѡ҆бѣща́вый,

O Christ God, trampling down death by death: Thou Who art one of the Holy Trinity, glorified together with the Father and the Holy Spirit, save us.

Deacon: Again and again, in peace let us pray to the Lord.

Choir: Lord, have mercy.

Deacon: Help us, save us, have mercy on us, and keep us, O God, by Thy grace.

Choir: Lord, have mercy.

Deacon: Calling to remembrance our most holy, most pure, most blessed, glorious Lady Theotokos and Ever-Virgin Mary, with all the saints, let us commit ourselves and one another and all our life unto Christ, our God.

Choir: To Thee, O Lord.

The priest secretly says the prayer of the third antiphon:

O Thou Who hast bestowed upon us these common and concordant prayers, and Who hast promised that when two or three are agreed in Thy name Thou

са́мъ и҆ ны́нѣ ра́бъ твои́хъ прошє́нїѧ къ поле́зномꙋ и҆спо́лни, пода́ѧ на́мъ въ настоѧ́щемъ вѣ́цѣ позна́нїе твоеѧ̀ и҆́стины, и҆ въ бꙋ́дꙋщемъ живо́тъ вѣ́чный да́рꙋѧ.

Возглаше́нїе: Ꙗ҆́кѡ бл҃гъ и҆ чл҃вѣколю́бецъ бг҃ъ є҆сѝ, и҆ тебѣ̀ сла́вꙋ возсыла́емъ, ѻ҆ц҃ꙋ, и҆ сн҃ꙋ, и҆ ст҃о́мꙋ дх҃ꙋ, ны́нѣ и҆ при́снѡ, и҆ во вѣ́ки вѣкѡ́въ.

Ли́къ: А҆ми́нь.

Здѣ̀ ѿверза́ютсѧ двє́ри на
ма́лый вхо́дъ.

Во цр҃твїи твое́мъ помѧнѝ на́съ, гдⷭ҇и, є҆гда̀ прїи́деши во цр҃твїи твое́мъ.

Бл҃же́ни ни́щїи дꙋ́хомъ, ꙗ҆́кѡ тѣ́хъ є҆́сть цр҃тво нбⷭ҇ное.

Бл҃же́ни пла́чꙋщїи, ꙗ҆́кѡ ті́и ѹ҆тѣ́шатсѧ.

Бл҃же́ни кро́тцыи, ꙗ҆́кѡ ті́и наслѣ́дѧтъ зе́млю.

Бл҃же́ни а҆́лчꙋщїи и҆ жа́ждꙋщїи пра́вды, ꙗ҆́кѡ ті́и насы́тѧтсѧ.

wouldst grant their requests: Do Thou Thyself fulfill the requests of Thy servants to their profit, granting us in this present age the knowledge of Thy truth, and in that to come, life everlasting.

Exclamation: For a good God art Thou and the Lover of mankind, and unto Thee do we send up glory, to the Father, and to the Son, and to the Holy Spirit, now and ever, and unto the ages of ages.

Choir: Amen.

> Here the doors are opened for the
> Small Entrance.

In Thy Kingdom remember us, O Lord, when Thou comest in Thy Kingdom.

Blessed are the poor in spirit, for theirs is the Kingdom of Heaven.

Blessed are they that mourn, for they shall be comforted.

Blessed are the meek, for they shall inherit the earth.

Blessed are they that hunger and thirst after righteousness, for they shall be filled.

Бл҃же́нни мл҃тивїи, ꙗ҆́кѡ ті́и поми́ловани бꙋ́дꙋтъ.

Бл҃же́нни чи́стїи се́рдцемъ, ꙗ҆́кѡ ті́и бг҃а оу҆́зрѧтъ.

Бл҃же́нни миротво́рцы, ꙗ҆́кѡ ті́и сы́нове бж҃їи нарекꙋ́тсѧ.

Бл҃же́нни и҆згна́ни пра́вды ра́ди, ꙗ҆́кѡ тѣ́хъ є҆́сть цр҃тво нб҃ное.

Бл҃же́нни є҆стѐ, є҆гда̀ поно́сѧтъ ва́мъ, и҆ и҆зженꙋ́тъ, и҆ рекꙋ́тъ всѧ́къ ѕо́лъ глаго́лъ, на вы̀ лжꙋ́ще менѐ ра́ди.

Ра́дꙋйтесѧ и҆ весели́тесѧ, ꙗ҆́кѡ мзда̀ ва́ша мно́га на нб҃сѣ́хъ.

Сла́ва ѻ҆ц҃ꙋ̀, и҆ сн҃ꙋ, и҆ ст҃о́мꙋ дх҃ꙋ.

И҆ ны́нѣ и҆ при́снѡ, и҆ во вѣ́ки вѣкѡ́въ. А҆ми́нь.

Пѣва́емꙋ же тре́тїемꙋ а҆нтїфѡ́нꙋ ѿ пѣвцє́въ, и҆лѝ бл҃же́ннамъ, а҆́ще є҆́сть недѣ́лѧ, є҆гда̀ прїи́дꙋтъ на Сла́ва: сщ҃е́нникъ и҆ дїа́конъ, ста́вше пред ст҃о́ю трапе́зою, творѧ́тъ покло́ны трѝ. Та́же прїе́мъ сщ҃е́нникъ ст҃о́е є҆ѵⷢ҇лїе, дае́тъ дїа́конꙋ, и҆ и҆дꙋ́тъ ѿ десны́ѧ страны̀ созадѝ пртⷭ҇о́ла,

Blessed are the merciful, for they shall obtain mercy.

Blessed are the pure in heart, for they shall see God.

Blessed are the peacemakers, for they shall be called sons of God.

Blessed are they that are persecuted for righteousness' sake, for theirs is the Kingdom of Heaven.

Blessed are ye when men shall revile you and persecute you, and shall say all manner of evil against you falsely for My sake.

Rejoice and be exceeding glad, for great is your reward in the Heavens.

Glory to the Father, and to the Son, and to the Holy Spirit.

Both now and ever, and unto the ages of ages. Amen.

As the Beatitudes (if it be Sunday) or the third antiphon is sung by the choir, when they come to the Glory, the priest and the deacon, standing before the Holy Table, make three bows from the waist. Then the priest, taking the Holy Gospel, gives

и҆ та́кѡ и҆зше́дше сѣ́верною страно́ю, предидꙋ́щымъ и҆̀мъ лампа́дамъ, творѧ́тъ ма́лый вхо́дъ, и҆ ста́вше на ѻ҆бы́чнѣмъ мѣ́стѣ, приклонѧ́ютъ ѻ҆́ба главы̀, и҆ дїа́конꙋ ре́кшꙋ: Гдꙋ помо́лимсѧ, глаго́летъ сщ҃е́нникъ моли́твꙋ вхо́да та́йнѡ.

Мл҃тва вхо́да:

Влⷣко гдⷭ҇и бж҃е на́шъ, ѹ҆ста́вивый на нб҃сѣ́хъ чи́ны и҆ во́инства а҆́гг҃лъ и҆ а҆рха́гг҃лъ въ слꙋже́нїе твоеѧ̀ сла́вы, сотворѝ со вхо́домъ на́шимъ вхо́дꙋ ст҃ы́хъ а҆́гг҃лѡвъ бы́ти, сослꙋжа́щихъ на́мъ, и҆ сославосло́вѧщихъ твою̀ бл҃гость.

Ꙗ҆́кѡ подоба́етъ тебѣ̀ всѧ́каѧ сла́ва, че́сть и҆ поклоне́нїе, ѻ҆ц҃ꙋ̀, и҆ сн҃ꙋ, и҆ ст҃о́мꙋ дх҃ꙋ, ны́нѣ и҆ при́снѡ, и҆ во вѣ́ки вѣкѡ́въ. А҆ми́нь.

Моли́твѣ же сконча́вшейсѧ, глаго́летъ дїа́конъ ко сщ҃е́нникꙋ, показꙋ́ѧй къ

it to the deacon, and they go to the right, behind the Holy Table. Thus coming out of the north side, with candles going before them, they make the Small Entrance; and standing in the usual place, both of them bow their heads, and the deacon, having said: Let us pray to the Lord, the priest says the prayer of the Entrance secretly:

The Prayer of the Entrance:

O Master Lord our God, Who hast appointed in the heavens the ranks and hosts of angels and archangels unto the service of Thy glory: With our entry do Thou cause the entry of the holy angels, serving and glorifying Thy goodness with us.

For unto Thee is due all glory, honor, and worship: to the Father, and to the Son, and to the Holy Spirit, now and ever, and unto ages of ages. Amen.

When the prayer is ended, the deacon says to the priest, pointing toward the east with

восто́кꙋ десни́цею, держа̀ вкꙋ́пѣ и҆ ѻ҆ра́рь тремѝ пе́рсты:

Бл҃гословѝ, влады́ко, ст҃ы́й вхо́дъ.

И҆ сщ҃е́нникъ, бл҃гословлѧ́ѧ, глаго́летъ:

Бл҃гослове́нъ вхо́дъ ст҃ы́хъ твои́хъ, всегда̀, ны́нѣ и҆ при́снѡ, и҆ во вѣ́ки вѣкѡ́въ.

Посе́мъ ѿхо́дитъ ко ст҃и́телю, и҆лѝ и҆гꙋ́менꙋ, дїа́конъ, и҆ цѣлꙋ́етъ є҆ѵⷢ҇лїе, а҆́ще предстои́тъ: а҆́ще же нѝ, цѣлꙋ́етъ сїѐ сщ҃е́нникъ.

И҆спо́лньшꙋсѧ же коне́чномꙋ тропарю̀, вхо́дитъ дїа́конъ посредѣ̀, и҆ ста́въ пред̾ і҆ере́емъ возвыша́етъ ма́лѡ рꙋ́цѣ, и҆ показꙋ́ѧй ст҃о́е є҆ѵⷢ҇лїе, глаго́летъ велегла́снѡ:

Премꙋ́дрость, про́сти.

Та́же поклони́всѧ, са́мъ же и҆ сщ҃е́нникъ созадѝ є҆гѡ̀, вхо́дитъ во ст҃ы́й ѻ҆лта́рь: и҆ дїа́конъ ᲂу҆́бѡ полага́етъ ст҃о́е є҆ѵⷢ҇лїе на ст҃ѣ́й трапе́зѣ.

his right hand, holding therein his orarion
with three fingers:

Bless, master, the holy entrance.

And the priest, blessing, says:

**Blessed is the entrance of Thy saints, always,
now and ever, and unto the ages of ages.**

After that, the deacon goes to the bishop,
or to the abbot (if either is present), and he
kisses the Gospel; if not, the priest kisses it.

When the prayer has been finished, the
deacon goes to the center, and standing in
front of the priest, lifts the Holy Gospel up
to be seen by all, and says in a loud voice:

Wisdom, aright!

Then, having bowed, as does the priest
behind him, the deacon and the priest
enter into the holy altar; and the deacon
immediately lays the Holy Gospel on the
Holy Table.

Пѣвцы̀ же пою́тъ:

Прїиди́те, поклони́мсѧ и҆ припаде́мъ ко хрⷭ҇тꙋ̀. Сп҃сѝ ны, сн҃е бж҃їй, во ст҃ы́хъ ди́венъ сы́й, пою́щыѧ тѝ: а҆ллилꙋ́їа. [є҆ди́ножды]

А҆́ще же недѣ́лѧ: Воскресы́й и҆з̾ ме́ртвыхъ, пою́щыѧ тѝ: а҆ллилꙋ́їа. [є҆ди́ножды]

Та́же, ѻ҆бы́чныѧ тропарѝ.

Глаго́летъ і҆ере́й моли́твꙋ сїю̀ та́йнѡ:

Мл҃тва трист҃а́гѡ пѣ́нїѧ:

Б҃же ст҃ы́й, и҆́же во ст҃ы́хъ почива́яй, трист҃ы́мъ гла́сомъ ѿ серафі́мѡвъ воспѣва́емый и҆ ѿ херꙋві́мѡвъ славосло́вимый, и҆ ѿ всѧ́кїѧ нбⷭ҇ныѧ си́лы покланѧ́емый, и҆́же ѿ небытїѧ̀ во є҆́же бы́ти приведы́й всѧ́ческаѧ, созда́вый человѣ́ка по ѻ҆́бразꙋ твоемꙋ̀ и҆ по подо́бїю, и҆ всѧ́кимъ твои́мъ дарова́нїемъ ᲂу҆краси́вый, даѧ́й просѧ́щемꙋ премꙋ́дрость и҆ ра́зꙋмъ, и҆ не презира́яй согрѣша́ющагѡ, но полага́яй на сп҃се́нїе

And the choir sings:

O come, let us worship and fall down before Christ; O Son of God Who art wondrous in the saints, save us who chant unto Thee: Alleluia. [once]

On Sundays: Who didst rise from the dead, save us who chant unto Thee: Alleluia. [once]

Then the appointed troparia [and kontakia are sung by the choir]. The priest says this prayer secretly:

The Prayer of the Trisagion Hymn:

O Holy God, Who restest in the saints, Who art praised with the thrice-holy hymn by the Seraphim, and art glorified by the Cherubim, and art worshipped by all the heavenly hosts, Who from non-existence hast brought all things into being, Who hast created man according to Thine image and likeness, and hast adorned him with Thine every gift; Who givest wisdom and understanding to him that asketh, and Who

покаѧ́нїе, сподо́бивый на́съ, смире́нныхъ
и҆ недосто́йныхъ ра̑бъ твои́хъ, и҆ въ ча́съ
се́й ста́ти пред̾ сла́вою ст҃а́гѡ твоегѡ̀
же́ртвенника, и҆ до́лжное тебѣ̀ поклоне́нїе
и҆ славосло́вїе приноси́ти: са́мъ, влⷣко, прїими́
и҆ ѿ ѹ҆́стъ на́съ грѣ́шныхъ трист҃ꙋ́ю пѣ́снь,
и҆ посѣти́ ны бл҃гостїю твое́ю, прости́
на́мъ всѧ́кое согрѣше́нїе во́льное же и҆
нево́льное, ѡ҆свѧти́ на̑ша дꙋ́шы и҆ тѣлеса̀,
и҆ да́ждь на́мъ въ преподо́бїи слꙋжи́ти
тебѣ̀ всѧ̑ дни живота̀ на́шегѡ, мл҃твами
ст҃ы́ѧ бц҃ы, и҆ всѣ́хъ ст҃ы́хъ, ѿ вѣ́ка тебѣ̀
бл҃гоꙋгоди́вшихъ.

Є҆гда́ же пѣвцы̀ прїидꙋ́тъ въ послѣ́днїй
тропа́рь, гл҃етъ дїа́конъ ко і҆ере́ю, приклонѧ̀
вкꙋ́пѣ главꙋ̀, и҆ ѻ҆ра́рь въ рꙋцѣ̀ держа̀
тремѝ пе́рсты:

Бл҃гословѝ, влады́ко, вре́мѧ трист҃а́гѡ.

disdainest not him that sinneth, but hast appointed repentance unto salvation; Who hast vouchsafed us, Thy lowly and unworthy servants, to stand even in this hour before the glory of Thy holy altar, and to offer the worship and glory due unto Thee: Do Thou Thyself, O Master, accept even from the lips of us sinners the thrice-holy hymn, and visit us in Thy goodness. Pardon us every sin, voluntary and involuntary; sanctify our souls and bodies, and grant us to serve Thee in holiness all the days of our life, through the intercessions of the holy Theotokos, and of all the saints, who from the ages have been pleasing unto Thee.

And when the singers come to the last kontakion, the deacon says to the priest, while bowing his head and holding his orarion with three fingers of his right hand:

Bless, master, the time of the Thrice-holy.

Іере́й же, зна́менꙋѧ є҆гѡ̀,
глаго́летъ:

Ꙗ҆́кѡ ст҃ъ є҆сѝ, бж҃е на́шъ, и҆ тебѣ̀ сла́вꙋ возсыла́емъ, ѻ҆ц҃ꙋ, и҆ сн҃ꙋ, и҆ ст҃о́мꙋ дх҃ꙋ, ны́нѣ и҆ при́снѡ.

Сконча́вшꙋсѧ же тропарю̀, приходитъ дїа́конъ бли́зъ ст҃ы́хъ двере́й, и҆ показꙋ́ѧй ѻ҆раре́мъ, пе́рвѣе оу҆́бѡ ко і҆кѡ́нѣ хрⷭ҇то́вѣ, глаго́летъ:

Гдⷭ҇и, сп҃сѝ бл҃гочести́выѧ, и҆ оу҆слы́ши ны̀.

Та́же наво́дитъ, глаго́лѧ ко внѣ̀ стоѧ́щымъ велегла́снѡ:

И҆ во вѣ́ки вѣкѡ́въ.
Ли́къ: А҆ми́нь и҆ Трист҃о́е.

Пѣва́емꙋ же трист҃о́мꙋ, глаго́лютъ и҆ са́ми, і҆ере́й же и҆ дїа́конъ, трист҃о́е: творѧ́ще вкꙋ́пѣ и҆ покло́ны трѝ пред ст҃о́ю трапе́зою.

Та́же глаго́летъ дїа́конъ ко і҆ере́ю:

And the priest, signing him with the sign of
the Cross, exclaims:

**For holy art Thou, our God, and unto Thee
do we send up glory, to the Father, and to the
Son, and to the Holy Spirit, now and ever.**

And the kontakion having ended, the
deacon comes out through the holy doors,
and standing on the ambo and pointing
with his orarion, first to the icon of Christ,
says:

O Lord, save the pious, and hearken unto us.

Then he points to all the people, saying in a
loud voice:

And unto the ages of ages.

Choir: **Amen** and the Trisagion.

While the Trisagion is sung, both the
priest and the deacon themselves say the
Trisagion Hymn, together making three
bows before the Holy Table.

Then the deacon says to the priest:

Повели́, влады́ко.

И҆ ѿхо́дѧтъ къ го́рнемꙋ мѣ́стꙋ: и҆
сщ҃е́нникъ ѿхода̀ глаго́летъ:

Бл҃гослове́нъ грѧды́й во и҆́мѧ гдⷭ҇не.

Дїа́конъ: Бл҃гословѝ, влады́ко, го́рнїй
прⷭ҇то́лъ.

І҆ере́й же: Бл҃гослове́нъ є҆сѝ на прⷭ҇то́лѣ сла́вы
црⷭ҇твїѧ твоегѡ̀, сѣдѧ́й на херꙋві́мѣхъ,
всегда̀, ны́нѣ и҆ при́снѡ, и҆ во вѣ́ки вѣкѡ́въ.

[Вѣ́дательно, ꙗ҆́кѡ сщ҃е́нникꙋ не подоба́етъ
на го́рнее мѣ́сто восходи́ти, нижѐ сѣдѣ́ти
на не́мъ: но сѣдѣ́ти во странѣ̀ го́рнагѡ
прⷭ҇то́ла, и҆з̾ ю҆́жныѧ страны̀.]

И҆ по и҆сполне́нїи трист҃а́гѡ, дїа́конъ,
прише́дъ пред̾ ст҃ы́ѧ две́ри,
глаго́летъ:

Во́нмемъ.

І҆ере́й же возглаша́етъ: Ми́ръ всѣ́мъ.

И҆ чте́цъ глаго́летъ: И҆ дꙋ́хови твоемꙋ̀.

И҆ дїа́конъ па́ки: Премꙋ́дрость.

Command, master.

And they proceed to the high place; and
the priest, as he goes, says:

Blessed is He that cometh in the name of
the Lord.
Deacon: Bless, master, the high throne.
Priest: Blessed art Thou on the throne of
the glory of Thy kingdom, Thou that sittest
upon the Cherubim, always, now and ever,
and unto the ages of ages.

[It is to be noted that it is not proper for
the priest to go up onto the high place, nor
to sit thereon, but to sit on the south side of
the high throne.]

And upon the conclusion of the Trisagion,
the deacon, having come toward the holy
doors, says:

Let us attend.
Priest: Peace be unto all.
  Reader: And to thy spirit.
Deacon: Wisdom.

Й чтецъ: прокіменъ,
ѱаломъ дв҃довъ.

Посемъ діаконъ: Премꙋдростъ.

Й чтецъ надписаніе а҃пла: Дѣѧній ст҃ыхъ
а҃плъ чтеніе, йлѝ: Соборнагѡ посланіѧ
іаковлѧ, йлѝ петрова чтеніе, йлѝ
Къ римлѧнѡмъ, йлѝ Къ корінѳѧнѡмъ,
йлѝ Къ галатѡмъ посланіѧ ст҃агѡ а҃пла
павла чтеніе.

Й паки діаконъ: Вонмемъ.

А҃плꙋ же исполньшꙋсѧ,
глаголетъ сщ҃енникъ:

Миръ тѝ.
Й чтецъ: Й дꙋхови твоемꙋ.
Діаконъ: Премꙋдростъ.
Й чтецъ: Аллилꙋіа со стїхѝ.

Аллилꙋіа же пѣваемꙋ, й пріемъ діаконъ
кадильницꙋ й дѵміамъ, приходитъ къ
сщ҃енникꙋ, й пріемъ бл҃гословеніе ѿ негѡ,

And the reader says the prokeimenon from the Psalms of David.

And then the deacon: **Wisdom!**

And the reader, the title of the Epistle: **The Reading is from the Acts of the holy Apostles,** or **from the Catholic Epistle of the holy Apostle James,** or **of Peter,** or **from the Epistle of the holy Apostle Paul to the Romans,** or **to the Corinthians,** or **to the Galatians,** etc.

And again the deacon: **Let us attend.**

And when the Epistle is concluded, the priest says:

Peace be unto thee.

Reader: **And to thy spirit.**

Deacon: **Wisdom.**

Reader: **Alleluia** and its verses.

While the Alleluia is being chanted, the deacon, taking the censer and incense, approaches the priest, and taking a blessing

кади́тъ стꙋ́ю трапе́зꙋ ѻ҆́крестъ, и҆ ѻ҆лта́рь
ве́сь, и҆ сще́нника.

Сщⷨе́нникъ же глаго́летъ мⷧ҇твꙋ сїю та́йнѡ:

Мⷧ҇тва пре́жде є҆ѵⷢ҇лїа:

В҆озсїѧ́й въ сердца́хъ на́шихъ, чл҃вѣ́ко-
лю́бче вⷧ҇ко, твоегѡ̀ бг҃оразꙋ́мїѧ
нетлѣ́нный свѣ́тъ, и҆ мы́сленныѧ на́ши
ѿве́рзи ѻ҆́чи, во є҆ѵⷢ҇льскихъ твои́хъ
проповѣ́данїй разꙋмѣ́нїе: вложѝ въ на́съ
и҆ стра́хъ бл҃же́нныхъ твои́хъ за́повѣдей,
да плотскі́ѧ по́хѡти всѧ̀ попра́вше,
дꙋхо́вное жи́тельство про́йдемъ, всѧ̀, ꙗ҆̀же
ко бл҃гоꙋгожде́нїю твоемꙋ̀, и҆ мꙋ́дрствꙋюще
и҆ дѣ́юще. Ты́ бо є҆сѝ просвѣще́нїе дꙋ́шъ
и҆ тѣле́съ на́шихъ, хрⷭ҇тѐ бж҃е: и҆ тебѣ̀
сла́вꙋ возсыла́емъ, со безнача́льнымъ
твои́мъ ѻ҆ц҃е́мъ, и҆ прест҃ы́мъ и҆ бл҃ги́мъ и҆
животворѧ́щимъ твои́мъ дх҃омъ, ны́нѣ и҆
при́снѡ, и҆ во вѣ́ки вѣкѡ́въ. А҆ми́нь.

from him, censes the Holy Table round about, and the whole altar, and the priest.

And the priest says this prayer silently:

The Prayer Before the Gospel:

Shine forth within our hearts the incorruptible light of Thy knowledge, O Master, Lover of mankind, and open the eyes of our mind to the understanding of the preaching of Thy Gospel. Instill in us also the fear of Thy blessed commandments, that, trampling down all lusts of the flesh, we may pursue a spiritual way of life, being mindful of and doing all that is well-pleasing unto Thee. For Thou art the enlightenment of our souls and bodies, O Christ our God, and unto Thee do we send up glory, together with Thine unoriginate Father, and Thy Most-holy and good and life-creating Spirit, now and ever, and unto the ages of ages. Amen.

Дїа́конъ же, кади́льницꙋ ѿложи́въ на ѻбы́чное мѣ́сто, прихо́дитъ къ сщⷽе́нникꙋ, и̑ подклони́въ є̑мꙋ̀ главꙋ̀ свою̀, держа̀ и̑ ѻ̑ра́рь со стⷶы́мъ є̑ѵⷢлїемъ кра́йними пе́рсты, си́рѣчь, во ѻ́номъ мѣ́стѣ стⷶы́я трапе́зы, глаго́летъ:

Блгⷭвѝ, влады́ко, блгⷬвѣсти́теля стⷶа́гѡ а̑пⷭла и̑ є̑ѵⷢлі́ста и̑мⷦ҇.

Сщⷽе́нникъ, зна́менꙋꙗ̑ є̑го̀, глаго́летъ:

Бгⷭъ, млⷮтвами стⷶа́гѡ сла́внагѡ, всехва́льнагѡ а̑пⷭла и̑ є̑ѵⷢлі́ста и̑мⷦ҇, да да́стъ тебѣ̀ глаго́лъ блгⷬвѣствꙋ́ющемꙋ си́лою мно́гою, во и̑сполне́нїе є̑ѵⷢлі́а возлю́бленнагѡ сⷩа своегѡ̀, гдⷭа на́шегѡ і̑и̑са хрⷭта̀.

Дїа́конъ же ре́къ: А̑ми́нь, и̑ поклони́всѧ стⷶо́мꙋ є̑ѵⷢлі́ю, во́зметъ є̑̀, и̑ и̑зше́дъ стⷶы́ми две́рьми, предходѧ́щымъ є̑мꙋ̀ лампа́дамъ, прихо́дитъ и̑ сто́итъ

The deacon, having put away the censer in the usual place, approaches the priest, and bowing his head to him, holding the Holy Gospel with his orarion in the tips of his fingers, i.e., on that place of the Holy Table says:

Bless, master, him that proclaimeth the Good Tidings of the holy Apostle and Evangelist N..

The priest, signing him with the sign of the Cross, says:

May God, through the prayers of the holy, glorious, all-praised Apostle and Evangelist N., give speech with great power unto thee that bringest good tidings, unto the fulfillment of the Gospel of His beloved Son, our Lord Jesus Christ.

And the deacon having said: **Amen**, and having venerated the Holy Gospel, takes it, and goes out through the holy doors, candles preceding him, and goes

на а́мвѡ́нѣ, и҆лѝ на ѹ҆чине́ннѣмъ
мѣ́стѣ.

Ꙇ҆ере́й же, сто́ѧ пред̾ ст҃ою трапе́зою и҆ зрѧ̀
къ за́падꙋ, возглаша́етъ:

Премꙋ́дрость, про́сти, ѹ҆слы́шимъ ст҃а́гѡ
е҆ѵⷢ҇лїа. Та́же: Ми́ръ всѣ́мъ.
  Лю́дїе: И҆ дꙋ́хови твоемꙋ̀.
  Дїа́конъ: Ѿ и҆́мⷦ҇къ ст҃а́гѡ е҆ѵⷢ҇лїа чте́нїе.
  Ли́къ: Сла́ва тебѣ̀, гдⷭ҇и, сла́ва тебѣ̀.
  Сщ҃е́нникъ: Во́нмемъ.

  А҆́ще же сꙋ́ть два̀ дїа́кона, то є҆ди́нъ да
глаго́летъ: Премꙋ́дрость, про́сти. Та́же, и҆:
Во́нмемъ.

  И҆ и҆спо́лнившꙋсѧ е҆ѵⷢ҇лїю, глаго́летъ
сщ҃е́нникъ:

Ми́ръ тѝ бл҃говѣствꙋ́ющемꙋ.
  Ли́къ: Сла́ва тебѣ̀, гдⷭ҇и, сла́ва тебѣ̀.

forth and stands on the ambo, or on the
appointed place.

And the priest, standing before the Holy
Table and looking toward the west,
exclaims:

Wisdom. Aright! Let us hear the holy Gos-
pel. Then: Peace be unto all.
People: And to thy spirit.
Deacon: The reading is from the holy Gos-
pel according to N..
Choir: Glory to Thee, O Lord, glory to Thee.
Priest: Let us attend.

If there be two deacons, one may say:
Wisdom. Aright! then also Let us attend.

When the Gospel is concluded, the priest
says:

Peace be unto thee that bringest Good Tidings.
Choir: Glory to Thee, O Lord, glory to Thee.

И҆ ѿше́дъ дїа́конъ да́же до ст҃ы́хъ
двере́й, ѿдае́тъ ст҃о́е є҆ѵⷢ҇лїе сщ҃е́нникꙋ, и҆
затворѧ́ютсѧ па́ки свѧты́ѧ две́ри.

Дїа́конъ, ста́въ на ѻ҆бы́чномъ мѣ́стѣ,
начина́етъ си́це:

Рце́мъ вси̑ ѿ всеѧ̀ дꙋши̑, и҆ ѿ всегѡ̀
помышле́нїѧ на́шегѡ рце́мъ.

Ли́къ: Гдⷭ҇и, поми́лꙋй.

Дїа́конъ: Гдⷭ҇и вседержи́телю, бж҃е ѻ҆те́цъ
на́шихъ, мо́лимъ ти сѧ, ᲂу҆слы́ши и҆
поми́лꙋй.

Ли́къ: Гдⷭ҇и, поми́лꙋй.

Дїа́конъ: Поми́лꙋй на́съ, бж҃е, по вели́цѣй
ми́лости твое́й, мо́лимъ ти сѧ, ᲂу҆слы́ши
и҆ поми́лꙋй.

Ли́къ: Гдⷭ҇и, поми́лꙋй, три́жды.

Дїа́конъ: Є҆щѐ мо́лимсѧ ѡ҆ вели́комъ гос-
поди́нѣ и҆ ѻ҆тцѣ̀ на́шемъ свѧтѣ́йшемъ
патрїа́рсѣ и҆́мⷦ҇къ, и҆ ѡ҆ господи́нѣ на́шемъ
высокопреѡсщ҃е́ннѣйшемъ митрополи́тѣ
и҆́мⷦ҇къ, первоїера́рсѣ рꙋ́сскїѧ зарꙋбе́жныѧ

And the deacon goes to the holy doors, and gives the Holy Gospel to the priest, and the holy doors are closed again.

The deacon, standing in the usual place, begins thus:

Let us all say with our whole soul and with our whole mind, let us say:

Choir: Lord, have mercy.

Deacon: O Lord Almighty, the God of our Fathers, we pray Thee, hearken and have mercy.

Choir: Lord, have mercy.

Deacon: Have mercy on us, O God, according to Thy great mercy, we pray Thee, hearken and have mercy.

Choir: Lord, have mercy (thrice).

Deacon: Again we pray for our great lord and father, the Most Holy Patriarch N.; for our lord the Very Most Reverend Metropolitan N., First Hierarch of the Russian Church Abroad, for our lord the Most [or

цр҃кве, и ѡ господинѣ на́шемъ высоко_
преѡсщ҃е́ннѣйшемъ а҆рхїепкⷵпѣ [и҆лѝ
преѡсщ҃е́ннѣйшемъ е҆пкⷵпѣ] и҆мⷦ҇ъ, и ѡ
все́й во хрⷭ҇тѣ̀ бра́тїи на́шей.

Ли́къ: Гдⷭ҇и, поми́лꙋй, три́жды.

Сщ҃е́нникъ же глаго́летъ
мл҃твꙋ прилѣ́жнагѡ моле́нїѧ та́йнѡ:

Г дⷭ҇и бж҃е на́шъ, прилѣ́жное сїѐ моле́нїе
прїимѝ ѿ твои́хъ ра́бъ, и҆ помилꙋ́й на́съ
по мно́жествꙋ ми́лости твоеѧ̀, и҆ щедрѡ́ты
твоѧ̀ низпослѝ на ны̀, и҆ на всѧ̑ лю́ди твоѧ̑,
ча́ющыѧ ѿ тебѐ бога́тыѧ мл҃ти.

Дїа́конъ: Е҆щѐ мо́лимсѧ ѡ странѣ̀ се́й,
власте́хъ и҆ во́инствѣ е҆ѧ̀, и҆ всѣ́хъ вѣ́рою
и҆ бл҃гоче́стїемъ живꙋ́щихъ въ не́й.

Ли́къ: Гдⷭ҇и, поми́лꙋй, три́жды.

Дїа́конъ: Е҆щѐ мо́лимсѧ ѡ бг҃охрани́мѣй
странѣ̀ рѡссі́йстѣй и҆ правосла́вныхъ лю́дехъ
е҆ѧ̀ во ѻ҆те́чествїи и҆ разсѣѧ́нїи сꙋ́щихъ и҆
ѡ сп҃се́нїи и҆́хъ.

Ли́къ: Гдⷭ҇и, поми́лꙋй, три́жды.

Right] Reverend Archbishop [or Bishop] N.; and for all our brethren in Christ.

Choir: Lord, have mercy (thrice).

The priest says secretly the
Prayer of Fervent Supplication:

O Lord our God, accept this fervent supplication from Thy servants, and have mercy on us according to the multitude of Thy mercies, and send down Thy compassion upon us, and upon all Thy people that await of Thee abundant mercy.

Deacon: Again we pray for this land, its authorities and armed forces, and all who with faith and piety dwell therein.

Choir: Lord, have mercy (thrice).

Deacon: Again we pray for the God-preserved Russian land and its Orthodox people both in the homeland and the diaspora, and for their salvation.

Choir: Lord, have mercy (thrice).

Дїа́конъ: Є҆щѐ мо́лимсѧ гдⷭ҇ꙋ бг҃ꙋ на́шемꙋ ѡ҆ є҆́же и҆зба́вити лю́ди своѧ̀ ѿ вра̑гъ ви́димыхъ и҆ неви́димыхъ, въ на́съ же ѹ҆тверди́ти є҆диномы́сліе, братолю́біе и҆ бл҃гоче́стіе.

Ли́къ: Гдⷭ҇и, поми́лꙋй, три́жды.

Дїа́конъ: Є҆щѐ мо́лимсѧ ѡ҆ бра́тїахъ на́шихъ, сщ҃е́нницѣхъ, сщ҃енномона́сѣхъ, и҆ всѣ́мъ во хрⷭ҇тѣ̀ бра́тствѣ на́шемъ.

Ли́къ: Гдⷭ҇и, поми́лꙋй, три́жды.

Дїа́конъ: Є҆щѐ мо́лимсѧ ѡ҆ бл҃же́нныхъ и҆ приснопа́мѧтныхъ ст҃ѣ́йшихъ патрїа́рсѣхъ правосла́вныхъ, и҆ бл҃гочести́выхъ царѣ́хъ, и҆ бл҃говѣ́рныхъ цари́цахъ, и҆ созда́телехъ ст҃а́гѡ хра́ма сегѡ̀ [а҆́ще во ѻ҆би́тели: ст҃ы́ѧ ѻ҆би́тели сеѧ̀], и҆ ѡ҆ всѣ́хъ преждепочи́вшихъ ѻ҆тцѣ́хъ и҆ бра́тїахъ, здѣ̀ лежа́щихъ и҆ повсю́дꙋ, правосла́вныхъ.

Ли́къ: Гдⷭ҇и, поми́лꙋй, три́жды.

[Здѣ̀ прилага́ютсѧ прошє́нїѧ ѡ҆ болѧ́щихъ, ѡ҆ пꙋтешє́ствꙋющихъ, и҆ про́чаѧ.]

Deacon: Again we pray to the Lord our God that He may deliver His people from enemies, visible and invisible, and confirm in us oneness of mind, brotherly love, and piety.

Choir: Lord, have mercy (thrice).

Deacon: Again we pray for our brethren, the priests, the priestmonks, and all our brethren in Christ.

Choir: Lord, have mercy (thrice).

Deacon: Again we pray for the blessed and ever-memorable holy Orthodox patriarchs, and for pious kings and right-believing queens, and for the founders of this holy temple [if it be a monastery: this holy monastery], and for our fathers and brethren gone to their rest before us, and for all the Orthodox here and everywhere laid to rest.

Choir: Lord, have mercy (thrice).

[Here may be inserted various petitions as desired: see Petitions, page 277]

Дїа́конъ: Є҆щѐ мо́лимсѧ ѡ҆ плодоносѧ́щихъ и҆ добродѣ́ющихъ во ст҃ѣ́мъ и҆ всечестнѣ́мъ хра́мѣ се́мъ, трꙋжда́ющихсѧ, пою́щихъ и҆ предстоѧ́щихъ лю́дехъ, ѡ҆жида́ющихъ ѿ тебѐ вели́кїѧ и҆ бога́тыѧ мл҃ти.

Ли́къ: Гдⷭ҇и, поми́лꙋй, три́жды.

Возглаше́нїе: Ꙗ҆́кѡ мл҃тивъ и҆ чл҃вѣколю́бецъ бг҃ъ є҆сѝ, и҆ тебѣ̀ сла́вꙋ возсыла́емъ, ѻ҆ц҃ꙋ, и҆ сн҃ꙋ, и҆ ст҃о́мꙋ дх҃ꙋ, ны́нѣ и҆ при́снѡ, и҆ во вѣ́ки вѣкѡ́въ.

Ли́къ: А҆ми́нь.

А҆́ще ли бꙋ́детъ ѡ҆ ᲂу҆со́пшихъ приноше́нїе, дїа́конъ и҆лѝ сщ҃е́нникъ глаго́летъ є҆кте́нїю сїю̀:

Дїа́конъ: Поми́лꙋй на́съ, бж҃е, по вели́цѣй мл҃ти твое́й, мо́лимъ ти сѧ, ᲂу҆слы́ши и҆ поми́лꙋй.

Ли́къ: Гдⷭ҇и, поми́лꙋй, три́жды.

Дїа́конъ: Є҆щѐ мо́лимсѧ ѡ҆ ᲂу҆покое́нїи дꙋ́шъ ᲂу҆со́пшихъ рабѡ́въ бж҃їихъ и҆́мⷦ҇, и҆ ѡ҆ є҆́же

Deacon: Again we pray for them that bring offerings and do good works in this holy and all-venerable temple; for them that minister and them that chant, and for all the people here present that await of Thee great and abundant mercy.

Choir: Lord, have mercy (thrice).

Exclamation: For a merciful God art Thou and the Lover of mankind, and unto Thee do we send up glory, to the Father, and to the Son, and to the Holy Spirit, now and ever, and unto the ages of ages.

Choir: Amen.

If there be an offering for the departed, the deacon or priest says this litany :

Deacon: Have mercy on us, O God, according to Thy great mercy, we pray Thee, hearken and have mercy.

Choir: Lord, have mercy (thrice).

Deacon: Again we pray for the respose of the souls of the departed servants of God N.,

проститисѧ и́мъ всѧкомꙋ прегрѣше́нїю во́льномꙋ же и невольномꙋ.

Ли́къ: Гди, поми́лꙋй, три́жды.

Дїа́конъ: Ꙗ́кѡ да гдь бгъ оу҆чини́тъ дꙋшы и́хъ, и҆дѣ́же пра́веднїи оу҆покоѧ́ютсѧ.

Ли́къ: Гди, поми́лꙋй, три́жды.

Дїа́конъ: Ма́ти бжїѧ, цртва нбнагѡ, и ѡставле́нїѧ грѣхѡ́въ и́хъ, оу хрта̀ безсме́ртнагѡ црѧ̀ и бга на́шегѡ про́симъ.

Ли́къ: Пода́й, гди.

Дїа́конъ: Гдꙋ помо́лимсѧ.

Ли́къ: Гди, поми́лꙋй.

Сщенникъ глаго́летъ та́йнѡ:

Б҃же дꙋхѡ́въ и всѧ́кїѧ пло́ти, сме́рть попра́вый, и дїа́вола оу҆праздни́вый, и живо́тъ мі́рꙋ твоемꙋ̀ дарова́вый: са́мъ, гди, поко́й дꙋшы оу҆со́пшихъ ра́бъ твои́хъ и́мк, въ мѣ́стѣ свѣ́тлѣ, въ мѣ́стѣ ѕла́чнѣ, въ мѣ́стѣ поко́йнѣ, ѿню́дꙋже ѿбѣжѐ болѣ́знь, печа́ль и воздыха́нїе:

and that they may be forgiven every transgression, both voluntary and involuntary.

Choir: Lord, have mercy (thrice).

Deacon: That the Lord God commit their souls to where the righteous repose.

Choir: Lord, have mercy (thrice).

Deacon: The mercy of God, the kingdom of heaven, and the remission of their sins, let us ask of Christ, the immortal King and our God.

Choir: Grant this, O Lord.

Deacon: Let us pray to the Lord.

Choir: Lord, have mercy.

The priest says secretly:

O God of spirits and of all flesh, Who hast trampled down death, and overthrown the devil, and given life to Thy world: Do Thou Thyself, O Lord, give rest to the souls of Thy departed servants N., in a place of light, a place of green pasture, a place of repose, whence all sickness, sorrow,

всѧ́кое согрѣше́нїе содѣ́анное и́ми,
сло́вомъ, и́ли дѣ́ломъ, и́ли помышле́нїемъ,
ꙗ́кѡ бл҃гі́й чл҃вѣколю́бецъ бг҃ъ, прости́. ꙗ́кѡ
нѣ́сть человѣ́къ, и́же жи́въ бꙋ́детъ, и̇ не
согрѣши́тъ. ты̀ бо є҆ди́нъ кромѣ̀ грѣха̀,
пра́вда твоѧ̀ пра́вда во вѣ́ки, и̇ сло́во твоѐ
и́стина.

Возглаше́нїе: Ꙗ́кѡ ты̀ є҆сѝ воскр҃нїе
и̇ живо́тъ и̇ поко́й оу҆со́пшихъ ра́бъ
твои́хъ и́мⷬ҇къ, хрⷭ҇тѐ бж҃е на́шъ, и̇ тебѣ̀
сла́вꙋ возсыла́емъ, со безнача́льнымъ
твои́мъ ѻ҆ц҃е́мъ и̇ прест҃ы́мъ, и̇ бл҃ги́мъ, и̇
животворѧ́щимъ твои́мъ дх҃омъ, ны́нѣ
и̇ при́снѡ, и̇ во вѣ́ки вѣкѡ́въ.

Ли́къ: А҆ми́нь.

Та́же, дїа́конъ: Помоли́тесѧ, ѡ҆глаше́ннїи,
гдⷭ҇ви.

Ли́къ: Гдⷭ҇и, поми́лꙋй.

Дїа́конъ: Вѣ́рнїи, ѡ҆ ѡ҆глаше́нныхъ
помо́лимсѧ, да гдⷭ҇ь поми́лꙋетъ и́хъ.

Ли́къ: Гдⷭ҇и, поми́лꙋй.

and sighing are fled away. Pardon every sin committed by them in word, deed, or thought, in that Thou art a good God, the Lover of mankind; for there is no man that liveth and sinneth not, for Thou alone art without sin, Thy righteousness is an everlasting righteousness, and Thy word is truth. Exclamation: For Thou art the resurrection, and the life, and the repose of Thy departed servants N., O Christ our God, and unto Thee do we send up glory, together with Thine unoriginate Father, and Thy Mostholy and good and life-creating Spirit, now and ever, and unto the ages of ages.

Choir: Amen.

Then the deacon: Pray, ye catechumens, to the Lord.

Choir: Lord, have mercy.

Deacon: Ye faithful, let us pray for the catechumens that the Lord will have mercy on them.

Choir: Lord, have mercy.

Дїа́конъ: Ѿгласи́тъ и҆́хъ сло́вомъ и҆́стины.

Ли́къ: Гдⷭ҇и, поми́лꙋй.

Дїа́конъ: Ѿкры́етъ и҆́мъ є҆ѵⷢ҇лїе пра́вды.

Ли́къ: Гдⷭ҇и, поми́лꙋй.

Дїа́конъ: Соедини́тъ и҆́хъ ст҃ѣ́й свое́й собо́рнѣй и҆ а҆пⷭ҇льстѣ́й цр҃кви.

Ли́къ: Гдⷭ҇и, поми́лꙋй.

Дїа́конъ: Спⷭ҇и, поми́лꙋй, застꙋпѝ и҆ сохранѝ и҆́хъ, бж҃е, твое́ю блⷢ҇ода́тїю.

Ли́къ: Гдⷭ҇и, поми́лꙋй.

Дїа́конъ: Ѻ҆глаше́ннїи, главы̑ ва́шѧ гдⷭ҇ви приклони́те.

Ли́къ: Тебѣ̀, гдⷭ҇и.

Мл҃тва ѡ҆ ѡ҆глаше́нныхъ та́йнѡ глаго́летсѧ ѿ і҆ере́а:

Г‍дⷭ҇и бж҃е на́шъ, и҆́же на высо́кихъ живы́й и҆ на смире́нныѧ призира́ѧй, и҆́же сп҃се́нїе ро́дꙋ чл҃вѣ́ческомꙋ низпосла́вый, є҆диноро́днаго сн҃а твоегѡ̀ и҆ бг҃а, гдⷭ҇а на́шего і҆и҃са хрⷭ҇та̀: при́зри на рабы̑ твоѧ̑

Deacon: That He will catechize them with the word of truth.

Choir: Lord, have mercy.

Deacon: That He will reveal unto them the Gospel of righteousness.

Choir: Lord, have mercy.

Deacon: That He will unite them to His Holy, Catholic and Apostolic Church.

Choir: Lord, have mercy.

Deacon: Save them, have mercy on them, help them, and keep them, O God, by Thy grace.

Choir: Lord, have mercy.

Deacon: Ye catechumens, bow your heads unto the Lord.

Choir: To Thee, O Lord.

The priest secretly says the Prayer for the Catechumens:

O Lord our God, Who dwellest on high and lookest down on things that are lowly, Who unto the human race hast sent forth salvation, Thine Only-begotten Son and God, our Lord Jesus Christ: look upon

ѡглашє́нныѧ, подкло́ншыѧ тебѣ̀ своѧ̀ вы́ѧ, и҆ сподо́би а҆̀ во вре́мѧ бл҃гопотре́бное ба́ни пакибытїѧ̀, ѡ҆ставле́нїѧ грѣхѡ́въ и҆ ѻ҆де́жди нетлѣ́нїѧ, соединѝ и҆̀хъ ст҃ѣй твое́й собо́рнѣй и҆ а҆пⷭ҇льстѣй цр҃кви, и҆ сопричтѝ и҆̀хъ и҆збра́нномꙋ твоемꙋ̀ ста́дꙋ.

Возглаше́нїе: Да̀ и҆ ті́и съ на́ми сла́вѧтъ пречⷭ҇тное и҆ великолѣ́пое и҆́мѧ твоѐ, ѻ҆ц҃а̀, и҆ сн҃а, и҆ ст҃а́гѡ дх҃а, ны́нѣ и҆ прⷭ҇нѡ, и҆ во вѣ́ки вѣкѡ́въ.

Ли́къ: А҆ми́нь.

И҆ простира́етъ а҆нтїмі́нсъ сщ҃е́нникъ.

Дїа́конъ глаго́летъ: Е҆ли́цы ѡ҆глаше́ннїи, и҆зыди́те.

А҆́ще ли є҆́сть вторы́й дїа́конъ, возглаша́етъ и҆ то́й:

Ѡ҆глаше́ннїи, и҆зыди́те.

Та́же па́ки пе́рвый:

Thy servants, the catechumens, who have bowed their necks before Thee, and vouchsafe unto them at a seasonable time the laver of regeneration, the remission of sins, and the garment of incorruption; unite them to Thy Holy, Catholic, and Apostolic Church, and number them among Thy chosen flock. Exclamation: That they also with us may glorify Thy most honorable and majestic name: of the Father, and of the Son, and of the Holy Spirit, now and ever, and unto the ages of ages.

Choir: Amen.

And the priest spreads out the antimension.

Deacon: As many as are catechumens, depart.

If there be a second deacon, he exclaims this:

Catechumens, depart.

Then again the first deacon:

Е҆ли́цы ѡ҆глаше́ннїи, и҆зыди́те.

Да никто̀ ѿ ѡ҆глаше́нныхъ: е҆ли́цы вѣ́рнїи, па́ки и҆ па́ки ми́ромъ гдꙋ̀ помо́лимсѧ.

Ли́къ: Гдⷭ҇и, поми́лꙋй.

А҆́ще ли же е҆ди́нъ то́чїю і҆ере́й, тогда̀ глаго́летъ си́це:

Е҆ли́цы ѡ҆глаше́ннїи, и҆зыди́те, ѡ҆глаше́ннїи и҆зыди́те, е҆ли́цы ѡ҆глаше́ннїи и҆зыди́те: да никто̀ ѿ ѡ҆глаше́нныхъ, е҆ли́цы вѣ́рнїи, па́ки и҆ па́ки ми́ромъ гдꙋ̀ помо́лимсѧ.

Ли́къ: Гдⷭ҇и, поми́лꙋй.

Мⷧ҇тва вѣ́рныхъ, пе́рваѧ, та́йнѡ глаго́летсѧ ѿ і҆ере́а:

Б҃годари́мъ тѧ̀ гдⷭ҇и бж҃е си́лъ, сподо́бившаго на́съ предста́ти и҆ ны́нѣ ст҃о́мꙋ твоемꙋ̀ же́ртвенникꙋ, и҆ припа́сти ко щедро́тамъ твои́мъ ѡ҆ на́шихъ грѣсѣ́хъ, и҆ ѡ҆ лю́дскихъ невѣ́дѣнїихъ: прїимѝ бж҃е моле́нїе на́ше, сотвори́ ны досто́йны бы́ти,

As many as are catechumens, depart.

Let none of the catechumens remain. As many as are of the faithful: again and again, in peace let us pray to the Lord.

Choir: Lord, have mercy.

But if there be only a priest alone, then he says this:

As many as are catechumens, depart. Catechumens, depart. As many as are catechumens, depart: let none of the catechumens remain. As many as are of the faithful, again and again, in peace let us pray to the Lord.

Choir: Lord, have mercy.

The priest says secretly the First Prayer of the Faithful:

We thank Thee, O Lord God of hosts, Who hast vouchsafed us to stand even now before Thy Holy altar, and to fall down before Thy compassion for our sins, and for the errors of the people. Receive, O God, our supplication; make us to be worthy

є҆́же приноси́ти тебѣ̀ моле́нїѧ и̇ мольбы̀,
и̇ же́ртвы безкро́вныѧ ѿ всѣ́хъ люде́хъ
твои́хъ: и̇ ꙋ̇дово́ли на́съ, и̇̀хже положи́лъ
є̇сѝ въ слꙋже́бꙋ твою̀ сїю̀, си́лою дх҃а твоегѡ̀
ст҃а́гѡ, неѡ̇сꙋжде́ннѡ и̇ непреткнове́ннѡ
въ чи́стѣмъ свидѣ́тельствѣ со́вѣсти
на́шеѧ, призыва́ти тѧ̀ на всѧ́кое вре́мѧ
и̇ мѣ́сто: да послꙋ́шаѧ на́съ, ми́лостивъ
на́мъ бꙋ́деши, во мно́жествѣ твоеѧ̀
бл҃гости.

Дїа́конъ: Застꙋпѝ, сп҃сѝ, поми́лꙋй и̇ сохранѝ
на́съ, бж҃е, твое́ю бл҃года́тїю.

Ли́къ: Гдⷭ҇и, поми́лꙋй.

Дїа́конъ: Премꙋ́дрость.

Возглаше́нїе: Ꙗ̇́кѡ подоба́етъ тебѣ̀
всѧ́каѧ сла́ва, че́сть и̇ поклоне́нїе, ѻ̇ц҃ꙋ̀, и̇
сн҃ꙋ, и̇ ст҃о́мꙋ дх҃ꙋ, ны́нѣ и̇ при́снѡ, и̇ во
вѣ́ки вѣкѡ́въ.

Ли́къ: А̇ми́нь.

Дїа́конъ: Па́ки и̇ па́ки ми́ромъ гдⷭ҇ꙋ
помо́лимсѧ.

Ли́къ: Гдⷭ҇и, поми́лꙋй.

to offer unto Thee supplications and entreaties and bloodless sacrifices for all Thy people. And enable us whom Thou hast placed in Thy ministry, by the power of Thy Holy Spirit, without condemnation or faltering, with the clear witness of our conscience, to call upon Thee at all times and in every place, that, hearkening unto us, Thou mayest be gracious unto us in the multitude of Thy goodness.

Deacon: Help us, save us, have mercy on us, and keep us, O God, by Thy grace.

Choir: Lord, have mercy.

Deacon: Wisdom.

Exclamation: For unto Thee is due all glory, honor, and worship, to the Father, and to the Son, and to the Holy Spirit, now and ever, and unto the ages of ages.

Choir: Amen.

Deacon: Again and again, in peace let us pray to the Lord.

Choir: Lord, have mercy.

Е́гда̀ сщ҃е́нникъ є҆ди́нъ слꙋ́житъ,
сїѧ̀ не глаго́летъ:

Дїа́конъ: Ѡ҆ свы́шнемъ ми́рѣ, и҆ спⷭ҇е́нїи
дꙋ́шъ на́шихъ, гдꙋ̀ помо́лимсѧ.

Ли́къ: Гдⷭ҇и, поми́лꙋй.

Дїа́конъ: Ѡ҆ ми́рѣ всегѡ̀ мі́ра, бл҃госто ѧ́нїи
ст҃ы́хъ бж҃їихъ цр҃кве́й и҆ соедине́нїи всѣ́хъ,
гдꙋ̀ помо́лимсѧ.

Ли́къ: Гдⷭ҇и, поми́лꙋй.

Дїа́конъ: Ѡ҆ ст҃ѣ́мъ хра́мѣ се́мъ, и҆ съ
вѣ́рою, бл҃гоговѣ́нїемъ и҆ стра́хомъ бж҃їимъ
входѧ́щихъ во́нь, гдꙋ̀ помо́лимсѧ.

Ли́къ: Гдⷭ҇и, поми́лꙋй.

Дїа́конъ: Ѡ҆ и҆зба́витисѧ на́мъ ѿ всѧ́кїѧ
ско́рби, гнѣ́ва и҆ нꙋ́жды, гдꙋ̀ помо́лимсѧ.

Ли́къ: Гдⷭ҇и, поми́лꙋй.

Мл҃тва вѣ́рныхъ, втора́ѧ,
та́йнѡ глаго́летсѧ ѿ і҆ере́а:

Па́ки, и҆ мно́гажды тебѣ̀ припа́даемъ,
и҆ тебѣ̀ мо́лимсѧ, бл҃гі́й и҆ чл҃вѣколю́бче,

When a priest serves alone,
these are not said:

Deacon: For the peace from above, and the salvation of our souls, let us pray to the Lord.

Choir: Lord, have mercy.

Deacon: For the peace of the whole world, the good estate of the holy churches of God, and the union of all, let us pray to the Lord.

Choir: Lord, have mercy.

Deacon: For this holy temple, and for them that with faith, reverence, and fear of God enter herein, let us pray to the Lord.

Choir: Lord, have mercy.

Deacon: That we may be delivered from all tribulation, wrath, and necessity, let us pray to the Lord.

Choir: Lord, have mercy.

The priest says secretly the
Second Prayer of the Faithful:

Again and oftimes we fall down before Thee, and we pray Thee, O Good One

ꙗ́кѡ да призрѣ́въ на моле́нїе на́ше, ѡ҆чи́стиши на́шѧ дꙋ́шы и҆ тѣлеса̀ ѿ всѧ́кїѧ скве́рны пло́ти и҆ дꙋ́ха, и҆ да́си на́мъ неповинное и҆ неѡсꙋжде́нное предстоѧ́нїе ст҃а́гѡ твоегѡ̀ же́ртвенника. Да́рꙋй же, бж҃е, и҆ молѧ́щымсѧ съ на́ми преспѣ́анїе житїѧ̀ и҆ вѣ́ры и҆ ра́зꙋма дꙋхо́внагѡ: да́ждь и҆̀мъ всегда̀ со стра́хомъ и҆ любо́вїю слꙋжа́щымъ тебѣ̀, неповинн[ѡ] и҆ неѡсꙋжде́нн[ѡ] причасти́тисѧ ст҃ы́хъ твои́хъ та́инъ, и҆ нб҃нагѡ твоегѡ̀ цр҃т́вїѧ сподо́битисѧ.

Дїа́конъ: Застꙋпѝ, сп҃сѝ, поми́лꙋй и҆ сохранѝ на́съ, бж҃е, твое́ю бл҃года́тїю.

Ли́къ: Гд҃и, поми́лꙋй.

Дїа́конъ: Премꙋ́дрость.

Вхо́дитъ дїа́конъ сѣ́верными две́рьми.

Возглаше́нїе: Ꙗ́кѡ да под держа́вою твое́ю всегда̀ храни́ми, тебѣ̀ сла́вꙋ возсыла́емъ, ѻ҆ц҃ꙋ̀, и҆ сн҃ꙋ, и҆ ст҃о́мꙋ дх҃ꙋ, ны́нѣ и҆ при́снѡ, и҆ во вѣ́ки вѣкѡ́въ.

Ли́къ: А҆ми́нь.

and Lover of mankind, that, regarding our supplication, Thou wilt cleanse our souls and bodies of all defilement of flesh and spirit, and grant us to stand guiltless and uncondemned before Thy holy altar. Grant also, O God, to them that pray with us, advancement in life and faith, and spiritual understanding. Grant them ever to serve Thee with fear and love, and to partake, guiltless and uncondemned, of Thy Holy Mysteries, and to be vouchsafed Thy heavenly kingdom.

Deacon: Help us, save us, have mercy on us, and keep us, O God, by Thy grace.

Choir: Lord, have mercy.

Deacon: Wisdom.

The deacon enters through the north door.

Exclamation: That always being guarded under Thy dominion, we may send up glory unto Thee, to the Father, and to the Son, and to the Holy Spirit, now and ever, and unto the ages of ages.

Choir: Amen.

И ѿверза́ютсѧ ст҃ы́ѧ две́ри.

Та́же прїе́мъ дїа́конъ кади́льницꙋ, и ѳѷмїа́мъ вложи́въ, прихо́дитъ ко сщ҃е́нникꙋ, и прїе́мъ блⷮгослове́нїе ѿ негѡ̀, кади́тъ ст҃ꙋ́ю трапе́зꙋ ѻ҆́крестъ и҆ ѻ҆лта́рь ве́сь, и҆ сщ҃е́нника: глаго́летъ же и҆ н҃-й ѱало́мъ, и҆ тропарѝ ᲂу҆мили́тельныѧ, є҆ли́ка и҆зво́литъ.

Мл҃тва ю҆́же твори́тъ сщ҃е́нникъ въ себѣ̀, херꙋві́мской пѣ́сни пѣва́емѣй:

Н иктѡ́же досто́инъ ѿ свѧза́вшихсѧ плотски́ми похотьмѝ и сластьмѝ приходи́ти, и҆лѝ приближи́тисѧ, и҆лѝ слꙋжи́ти тебѣ̀, цр҃ю̀ сла́вы: є҆́же бо слꙋжи́ти тебѣ̀, вели́ко и҆ стра́шно и҆ самѣ́мъ нбⷭ҇нымъ си́лам. Но ѻ҆ба́че неизрече́ннагѡ ра́ди и҆ безмѣ́рнагѡ твоегѡ̀ чл҃вѣколю́бїѧ, непрело́жнѡ и҆ неизмѣ́ннѡ бы́лъ є҆сѝ чл҃вѣ́къ, и҆ а҆рхїере́й на́мъ бы́лъ є҆сѝ: и҆ слꙋже́бныѧ сеѧ̀ и҆ безкро́вныѧ же́ртвы

And the holy doors are opened.

Then the deacon, taking the censer and placing incense in it, approaches the priest, and, taking a blessing from him, censes around the Holy Table, and the whole altar, and the icons, and the priest, and the choir, and the people, saying Psalm 50 to himself, and the troparia of compunction, and whatsoever he may wish.

Whilst the Cherubic Hymn is being sung, the priest reads secretly this prayer:

None is worthy among them that are bound with carnal lusts and pleasures, to approach or to draw nigh, or to minister unto Thee, O King of glory, for to serve Thee is a great and fearful thing even unto the heavenly hosts themselves. Yet because of Thine ineffable and immeasurable love for mankind, without change or alteration Thou didst become man, and didst become our High Priest, and didst deliver unto us

сщеннодѣйствїе преда́лъ є҆сѝ на́мъ, ꙗ҆́кѡ
влⷣка всѣ́хъ: ты́ бо є҆ди́нъ, гдⷭ҇и бж҃е на́шъ,
влⷣчествꙋеши нбⷭ҇ными и҆ земны́ми, и҆́же
на прⷭ҇то́лѣ херꙋві́мстѣ носи́мый, и҆́же
серафі́мѡвъ гдⷭ҇ь, и҆ цр҃ь і҆и҃левъ, и҆́же є҆ди́нъ
ст҃ъ, и҆ во ст҃ы́хъ почива́ѧй. Та̀ ᲂу҆́бо молю̀
є҆ди́наго бл҃га́го и҆ бл҃гопослꙋшли́ваго:
при́зри на мѧ̀ грѣ́шнаго и҆ непотре́бнаго
раба̀ твоего̀, и҆ ѡ҆чи́сти мою̀ дꙋ́шꙋ и҆ се́рдце
ѿ со́вѣсти лꙋка́выѧ, и҆ ᲂу҆дови́ мѧ, си́лою
ст҃а́гѡ твоегѡ̀ дх҃а, ѡ҆блече́нна бл҃года́тїю
сщ҃е́нства, предста́ти ст҃ѣ́й твое́й се́й
трапе́зѣ, и҆ сщеннодѣ́йствовати ст҃о́е и҆
пречⷭ҇тое твоѐ тѣ́ло и҆ чⷭ҇тнꙋ́ю кро́вь: къ
тебѣ̀ бо прихождꙋ̀ приклѡ́нь мою̀ вы́ю, и҆
молю́ ти сѧ, да не ѿврати́ши лица̀ твоегѡ̀
ѿ менѐ, нижѐ ѿри́неши менѐ ѿ ѻ҆́трѡкъ
твои́хъ: но сподо́би принесе́ннымъ тебѣ̀
бы́ти, мно́ю грѣ́шнымъ и҆ недосто́йнымъ

the ministry of this liturgical and bloodless sacrifice, for Thou art the Master of all. Thou alone, O Lord our God, dost rule over those in heaven and those on earth, art borne upon the throne of the Cherubim, art Lord of the Seraphim and King of Israel, Thou alone art holy and restest in the saints. I implore Thee, therefore, Who alone art good and inclined to listen: Look upon me Thy sinful and unprofitable servant, and purge my soul and heart of a wicked conscience, and by the power of Thy Holy Spirit, enable me, who am clothed with the grace of the priesthood, to stand before this Thy Holy Table, and to perform the sacred Mystery of Thy holy and immaculate Body and precious Blood. For unto Thee do I draw nigh, bowing my neck, and I pray Thee: Turn not Thy countenance away from me, neither cast me out from among Thy children, but vouchsafe that these gifts be offered unto Thee by me, Thy sinful and unworthy servant: for

рабѡмъ твои́мъ, дарѡ́мъ си́мъ: ты́ бо
є҆сѝ приносѧ́й и҆ приноси́мый, и҆ прїе́млѧй
и҆ раздава́емый, хрⷭ҇тѐ бже на́шъ, и҆ тебѣ̀
сла́вꙋ возсыла́емъ, со безнача́льнымъ
твои́мъ ѻ҆ц҃е́мъ, и҆ прест҃ы́мъ, и҆ бл҃ги́мъ, и҆
животворѧ́щимъ твои́мъ дх҃омъ, ны́нѣ и҆
при́снѡ, и҆ во вѣ́ки вѣкѡ́въ. А҆ми́нь.

И҆спо́лнившейсѧ же мл҃твѣ, глаго́лютъ
и҆ ті́и херꙋві́мскꙋю пѣ́снь, три́жды: по
ко́емждо же скончанїи, покланѧ́ютсѧ по
є҆ди́ноцїи.

Сщ҃е́нникъ: И҆̀же херꙋві́мы та́йнѡ ѡ҆бра_
зꙋ́юще, и҆ животворѧ́щей трⷪ҇цѣ трист҃ꙋ́ю
пѣ́снь припѣва́юще, всѧ́кое ны́нѣ
житє́йское ѿложи́мъ попече́нїе.
Дїа́конъ: Ꙗ҆́кѡ да цр҃ѧ̀ всѣ́хъ под̾и́мемъ,
а҆́гг҃льскими неви́димѡ дорꙋноси́ма чи́нми.
А҆ллилꙋ́їа, а҆ллилꙋ́їа, а҆ллилꙋ́їа.

Та́же ѿхо́дѧтъ въ предложе́нїе, предходѧ́щꙋ
дїа́конꙋ, и҆ кади́тъ і҆ере́й ст҃а̑ѧ, въ себѣ̀
молѧ́сѧ:

Thou art He that offereth and is offered, that accepteth and is distributed, O Christ our God, and unto Thee do we send up glory, together with Thine unoriginate Father, and Thy Most-holy, good and life-creating Spirit, now and ever, and unto the ages of ages. Amen.

When the prayer is completed, the priest and the deacon say also the Cherubic Hymn, thrice; and bowing once at the conclusion of each repetition.

Priest: Let us, who mystically represent the Cherubim and chant the thrice-holy hymn to the life-creating Trinity, now lay aside all earthly care.

Deacon: That we may receive the King of all, Who cometh invisibly upborne by the ranks of angels. Alleluia, alleluia, alleluia.

And the priest goes to the table of oblation after the deacon, and censes the holy things, praying quietly:

Бж҃е, ѡ҆чи́сти мѧ̀ грѣ́шнаго, три́жды.

Діа́конъ глаго́летъ ко сщ҃е́нникꙋ:

Возмѝ, влады́ко.

Й҆ сщ҃е́нникъ, взе́мъ воздꙋ́хъ, возлага́етъ
на лѣ́вое ра́мо є҆гѡ̀, глаго́лѧ:

Возми́те рꙋ́ки ва́шѧ во ст҃а́ѧ, и҆
бл҃гослови́те гд҃а.

Та́же ст҃ы́й ді́скосъ прїе́мъ, возлага́етъ на
главꙋ̀ дїа́кона, со всѧ́кимъ внима́нїемъ
и҆ бл҃гогове́нїемъ, и҆мѣ́ѧй вкꙋ́пѣ дїа́конъ
и҆ кади́льницꙋ на є҆ди́номъ ѿ пе́рстовъ
десны́ѧ рꙋкѝ. Са́мъ же ст҃ы́й поти́ръ въ
рꙋцѣ̀ прїе́млетъ: и҆ и҆схо́дѧтъ ѻ҆́ба сѣ́верною
страно́ю молѧ́щесѧ, предходѧ́щымъ и҆̀мъ
лампа́дамъ.

Діа́конъ глаго́летъ: Вели́каго господи́на и҆
ѻ҆тца̀ на́шего и҆̀мⷦъ, ст҃ѣ́йшаго патрїа́рха
моско́вскаго и҆ всеѧ̀ рꙋ́си, и҆ господи́на
на́шего высокопрешесщ҃е́ннѣйшаго и҆̀мⷦъ,
митрополі́та восто́чно-а҆мерика́нскаго

O God, cleanse me, a sinner. Thrice.

The deacon says to the priest:

Lift up, master.

And the priest, taking the aer, lays it upon the deacon's left shoulder, saying:

Lift up your hands in the sanctuary, and bless the Lord.

And taking the holy discos, he places it upon the deacon's head, with all attentiveness and reverence, the deacon having also the censer on one of his fingers of his right hand. The priest himself takes the holy chalice in his hands. They come out by the north door, preceded by the candle-bearers.

The deacon says: Our great lord and father N., the Most Holy Patriarch of Moscow and all Russia; our lord the Very Most Reverend N., Metropolitan of Eastern America and New York, First Hierarch of the

и҆ нью-ꙇ҆о́ркскагѡ, первоїера́рха рꙋ́сскїѧ
зарꙋбе́жныѧ цр҃кве, и҆ господи́на на́шегѡ,
высокопреѡсщⷭ҇е́ннѣйшагѡ и҆́мⷬ҇къ [и҆лѝ
преѡсщⷭ҇е́ннѣйшагѡ и҆́мⷬ҇къ], а҆рхїепⷭ҇кпа
[и҆лѝ є҆пⷭ҇кпа] [є҆гѡ́же є҆́сть ѻ҆́бласть], да
помѧне́тъ гдⷭ҇ь бг҃ъ во црⷭ҇твїи свое́мъ всегда̀,
ны́нѣ и҆ при́снѡ, и҆ во вѣ́ки вѣкѡ́въ.

Та́же сщ҃е́нникъ: Бг҃охрани́мꙋю странꙋ̀
рѡссі́йскꙋю и҆ правосла́вныѧ лю́ди є҆ѧ̀
во ѻ҆те́чествїи и҆ разсѣ́ѧнїи сꙋ́щыѧ, да
помѧне́тъ гдⷭ҇ь бг҃ъ во црⷭ҇твїи свое́мъ всегда̀,
ны́нѣ и҆ при́снѡ, и҆ во вѣ́ки вѣкѡ́въ.

Странꙋ̀ сїю̀, вла́сти и҆ во́инство є҆ѧ̀, и҆
вѣ́рою живꙋ́щихъ въ не́й, да помѧне́тъ
гдⷭ҇ь бг҃ъ во црⷭ҇твїи свое́мъ всегда̀, ны́нѣ и҆
при́снѡ, и҆ во вѣ́ки вѣкѡ́въ.

Сщ҃е́нство, мона́шество, всѣ́хъ гони́мыхъ
и҆ стра́ждꙋщихъ за вѣ́рꙋ правосла́внꙋю,
созда́телей, бл҃готвори́телей и҆ бра́тїю ст҃а́гѡ
хра́ма сегѡ̀ [и҆лѝ ст҃ы́ѧ ѻ҆би́тели сеѧ̀], и҆ всѣ́хъ
ва́съ правосла́вныхъ хрⷭ҇тїа́нъ, да помѧне́тъ
гдⷭ҇ь бг҃ъ во црⷭ҇твїи свое́мъ всегда̀, ны́нѣ и҆
при́снѡ, и҆ во вѣ́ки вѣкѡ́въ.

Russian Church Abroad; our lord the Most [or Right] Reverend N., Archbishop [or Bishop] of [name of diocese], may the Lord God remember in His Kingdom, always, now and ever, and unto the ages of ages.

Priest: The God-preserved Russian land and its Orthodox people both in the homeland and in the diaspora, may the Lord God remember in His kingdom, always, now and ever, and unto the ages of ages.

This land, its authorities, and armed forces, and all who with faith dwell therein, may the Lord God remember in His kingdom, always, now and ever, and unto the ages of ages.

The clergy, the monastics, all that are persecuted and suffer for the Orthodox Faith, the founders, benefactors, and the brotherhood of this holy temple (or holy monastery), and all of you Orthodox Christians, may the Lord God remember in His kingdom, always, now and ever, and unto the ages of ages.

Ли́къ: А҆ми́нь.

Вше́дъ же дїа́конъ вну́трь ст҃ы́хъ двере́й, стои́тъ ѡ҆десну́ю, и҆ хотѧ́щу сщ҃е́нникꙋ вни́ти, глаго́летъ къ немꙋ̀ дїа́конъ:

Да помѧне́тъ гд҃ь бг҃ъ сщ҃е́нство твоѐ во цр҃твїи свое́мъ.

И҆ сщ҃е́нникъ къ немꙋ̀:

Да помѧне́тъ гд҃ь бг҃ъ сщ҃еннодїа́конство твоѐ во цр҃твїи свое́мъ всегда̀, ны́нѣ и҆ при́снѡ, и҆ во вѣ́ки вѣкѡ́въ.

И҆ сщ҃е́нникъ ᲂу҆́бѡ поставлѧ́етъ ст҃ы́й потѝръ на ст҃у́ю трапе́зꙋ: ст҃ы́й же ді́скосъ взе́мъ со главы̀ дїа́кона, поставлѧ́етъ и҆ то́й на ст҃у́ю трапе́зꙋ, глаго́лѧ:

Бл҃гоѡбра́зный і҆ѡ́сифъ, съ дре́ва сне́мъ пречⷭ҇то́е твоѐ тѣ́ло, плащани́цею чи́стою ѡ҆бви́въ, и҆ бл҃гоꙋха́ньми во гро́бѣ но́вѣ закры́въ, положѝ.

Во гро́бѣ пло́тски, во а҆́дѣ же съ дш҃е́ю ꙗ҆́кѡ бг҃ъ, въ раѝ же съ разбо́йникомъ, и҆

Choir: **Amen.**

Having passed through the holy doors, the
deacon stands to the right; and as the priest
enters, the deacon says to him:

May the Lord God remember thy priesthood in His kingdom.

And the priest says to him:

May the Lord God remember thy sacred
diaconate in His kingdom, always, now and
ever, and unto the ages of ages.

And the priest places the holy chalice on
the Holy Table; and taking the holy diskos
from the head of the deacon, places it on
the Holy Table, saying:

The noble Joseph, having taken Thy most
pure Body down from the Tree and wrapped
It in pure linen and covered It with spices,
laid It in a new tomb.

In the grave bodily, but in Hades with
Thy soul as God; in Paradise with the thief,

на прⷭто́лѣ бы́лъ є҆сѝ, хрⷭтѐ, со ѻ҆ц҃е́мъ и҆ дх҃омъ, всѧ̀ и҆сполнѧ́ѧй неѡпи́санный.

Ꙗ҆́кѡ живоно́сецъ, ꙗ҆́кѡ раѧ̀ краснѣ́й_ шїй, вои́стиннꙋ и҆ всѧ́кагѡ черто́га ца́рскагѡ ꙗ҆ви́сѧ свѣтлѣ́йшїй, хрⷭтѐ, гро́бъ тво́й, и҆сто́чникъ на́шегѡ воскрⷭнїѧ.

Та́же покро́вцы ᲂу҆́бѡ взе́мъ ѿ сщ҃е́ннагѡ ді́скоса, и҆ ст҃а́гѡ поти́ра, полага́етъ на є҆ди́ной странѣ̀ ст҃ы́ѧ трапе́зы: возд(ꙋ)хъ же ѿ дїа́кона ра́ма взе́мъ, и҆ покади́въ покрыва́етъ и҆́мъ ст҃а̑ѧ, глаго́лѧ:

Бл҃гоѻбра́зный і҆ѡ́сифъ, съ дре́ва сне́мъ пречⷭтое твоѐ тѣ́ло, плащани́цею чи́стою ѡ҆бви́въ, и҆ бл҃гоꙋха́ньми во гро́бѣ но́вѣ закры́въ, положѝ.

И҆ прїе́мъ кади́льницꙋ ѿ дїа́коновы рꙋкѝ, кади́тъ ст҃а̑ѧ три́жды, глаго́лѧ:

and on the throne with the Father and the Spirit wast Thou Who fillest all things, O Christ the Inexpressible.

Thy tomb, the source of our resurrection, O Christ, hath appeared as life-bearing, as more beautiful than Paradise and truly more resplendent than any royal chamber.

Then taking the veils from the holy diskos and the holy chalice, the priest lays them to one side on the Holy Table; taking the aer from the deacon's shoulder, and having censed it, he covers the Holy Gifts with it, saying:

The noble Joseph, having taken Thy most pure Body down from the Tree and wrapped It in pure linen and covered It with spices, laid It in a new tomb.

And taking the censer from the hand of the deacon, the priest censes the Holy Gifts thrice, saying:

Оу҆блажи́, гдⷭ҇и, бл҃говоле́нїемъ твои́мъ сїѡ́на, и҆ да созижд́ꙋтсѧ стѣ́ны і҆е҆рⷧ҇имскі́ѧ: тогда̀ благоволи́ши же́ртвꙋ пра́вды, возноше́нїе и҆ всесожега́емаѧ, тогда̀ возложа́тъ на о҆лта́рь тво́й тельцы̀.

И҆ ѿда́въ кади́льницꙋ, и҆ ѡ҆пꙋсти́въ фелѡ́нь, приклони́въ же главꙋ́, глаго́летъ дїа́конꙋ:

Помоли́сѧ ѡ҆ мнѣ̀, бра́те и҆ сослꙋжи́телю.

И҆ дїа́конъ къ немꙋ́:

Дх҃ъ ст҃ы́й на́йдетъ на тѧ̀, и҆ си́ла вы́шнѧгѡ ѡ҆сѣни́тъ тѧ̀.

И҆ сщ҃е́нникъ: То́йже дх҃ъ содѣ́йствꙋетъ на́мъ всѧ̑ дни̑ живота̀ на́шегѡ.

Та́же и҆ дїа́конъ, поклони́въ и҆ са́мъ главꙋ́, держа̀ вкꙋ́пѣ и҆ ѻ҆ра́рь треми́ пе́рсты десни́цы, глаго́летъ ко сщ҃е́нникꙋ:

Помани́ мѧ, влⷣко ст҃ы́й.

O Lord, be favorable in Thy good will unto Zion, and let the walls of Jerusalem be builded up. Then shalt Thou be pleased with the sacrifice of righteousness, with oblation and whole-burnt offerings; then shall they offer young bullocks upon Thine altar.

And having returned the censer, and having bowed his head, the priest says to the deacon:

Pray for me, brother and concelebrant.

And the deacon says to him:

The Holy Spirit shall come upon thee, and the power of the Most High shall over-shadow thee.

And the priest: The same Spirit shall minister with us all the days of our life.

And the deacon, bowing his head himself and holding his orarion with the three fingers of his right hand, says to the priest:

Remember me, holy master.

Ѝ сщ҃е́нникъ: Да помѧне́тъ тѧ̀ гдⷭ҇ь бг҃ъ во црⷭ҇твїи свое́мъ всегда̀, нн҃ѣ и прⷭ҇нѡ, и во вѣ́ки вѣкѡ́въ.

Ѝ дїа́конъ: А҆ми́нь.

Ѝ цѣлова́въ десни́цꙋ сщ҃е́нника, и҆схо́дитъ дїа́конъ сѣ́верными две́рьми, и҆ ста́въ на ѻ҆бы́чномъ мѣ́стѣ, глаго́летъ:

И҆спо́лнимъ моли́твꙋ на́шꙋ гдⷭ҇ви.

Ли́къ: Гдⷭ҇и, поми́лꙋй.

Дїа́конъ: Ѡ҆ предложе́нныхъ чтⷭ҇ныхъ дарѣ́хъ, гдⷭ҇ꙋ помо́лимсѧ.

Ли́къ: Гдⷭ҇и, поми́лꙋй.

Дїа́конъ: Ѡ҆ ст҃ѣ́мъ хра́мѣ се́мъ, и҆ съ вѣ́рою, бл҃гоговѣ́нїемъ и҆ стра́хомъ бж҃їимъ входѧ́щихъ во́нь, гдⷭ҇ꙋ помо́лимсѧ.

Ли́къ: Гдⷭ҇и, поми́лꙋй.

Дїа́конъ: Ѡ҆ и҆зба́витисѧ на́мъ ѿ всѧ́кїѧ ско́рби, гнѣ́ва и҆ нꙋ́жды, гдⷭ҇ꙋ помо́лимсѧ.

Ли́къ: Гдⷭ҇и, поми́лꙋй.

And the priest: May the Lord God remember thee in His kingdom, always, now and ever, and unto the ages of ages.

Deacon: Amen.

And the deacon, having kissed the right hand of the priest, goes out the north door, and standing in the usual place, says:

Let us complete our prayer unto the Lord.

Choir: Lord, have mercy.

Deacon: For the precious Gifts set forth, let us pray to the Lord.

Choir: Lord, have mercy.

Deacon: For this holy temple, and for them that with faith, reverence, and fear of God enter herein, let us pray to the Lord.

Choir: Lord, have mercy.

Deacon: That we may be delivered from all tribulation, wrath, and necessity, let us pray to the Lord.

Choir: Lord, have mercy.

Мл҃тва проскоми́дїи, по поставле́нїи бжⷭ҇твенныхъ дарѡ́въ на ст҃ѣ́й трапе́зѣ та́йнѡ глаго́летсѧ ѿ і҆ере́а:

Гдⷭ҇и бж҃е вседержи́телю, є҆ди́не ст҃е, прїе́млѧй же́ртвꙋ хвале́нїѧ ѿ призыва́ющихъ тѧ̀ всѣ́мъ се́рдцемъ, прїими̏ и҆ на́съ грѣ́шныхъ моле́нїе и҆ принеси̏ ко ст҃о́мꙋ твоемꙋ̀ же́ртвенникꙋ, и҆ ѹ҆дово́ли на́съ приноси́ти тебѣ̀ да́ры же и҆ же́ртвы дꙋхѡ́вныѧ ѡ҆ на́шихъ грѣсѣ́хъ и҆ ѡ҆ людски́хъ невѣ́дѣнїихъ, и҆ сподо́би на́съ ѡ҆брѣсти̏ бл҃года́ть пред тобо́ю, є҆́же бы́ти тебѣ̀ бл҃гопрїѧ́тнꙋй же́ртвѣ на́шей, и҆ всели́тисѧ дх҃ꙋ бл҃года́ти твоеѧ̀ бл҃го́мꙋ въ на́съ, и҆ на предлежа́щихъ дарѣ́хъ си́хъ, и҆ на всѣ́хъ лю́дехъ твои́хъ.

Дїа́конъ: Застꙋпѝ, сп҃сѝ, поми́лꙋй и҆ сохранѝ на́съ, бж҃е, твое́ю бл҃года́тїю.

Ли́къ: Гдⷭ҇и, поми́лꙋй.

Дїа́конъ: Днѐ всегѡ̀ соверше́нна, ст҃а, ми́рна и҆ безгрѣ́шна, ѹ҆ гдⷭ҇а про́симъ.

The priest secretly says the Prayer of the Oblation, after placing the Divine Gifts on the Holy Table:

O Lord God Almighty, Who alone art holy, Who dost accept a sacrifice of praise from them that call upon Thee with their whole heart: accept also the supplication of us sinners, and bring it to Thy Holy Altar, and enable us to offer unto Thee both gifts and spiritual sacrifices for our sins and for the errors of the people, and vouchsafe us to find grace before Thee, that our sacrifice may be acceptable unto Thee, and that the good Spirit of Thy grace may rest upon us, and upon these Gifts set forth, and upon all Thy people.

Deacon: Help us, save us, have mercy on us, and keep us, O God, by Thy grace.

Choir: Lord, have mercy.

Deacon: That the whole day may be perfect, holy, peaceful, and sinless, let us ask of the Lord.

Ли́къ: Пода́й, гдⷭ҇н.

Дїа́конъ: А҆́гг҃ла ми́рна, вѣ́рна наста́вника, храни́телѧ дꙋ́шъ и҆ тѣле́съ на́шихъ, ᲂу҆ гдⷭ҇а про́симъ.

Ли́къ: Пода́й, гдⷭ҇н.

Дїа́конъ: Проще́нїѧ и҆ ѡ҆ставле́нїѧ грѣхѡ́въ и҆ прегрѣше́нїй на́шихъ, ᲂу҆ гдⷭ҇а про́симъ.

Ли́къ: Пода́й, гдⷭ҇н.

Дїа́конъ: До́брыхъ и҆ поле́зныхъ дꙋша́мъ на́шымъ, и҆ ми́ра мі́рови, ᲂу҆ гдⷭ҇а про́симъ.

Ли́къ: Пода́й, гдⷭ҇н.

Дїа́конъ: Про́чее вре́мѧ живота̀ на́шегѡ въ ми́рѣ и҆ покаѧ́нїи сконча́ти, ᲂу҆ гдⷭ҇а про́симъ.

Ли́къ: Пода́й, гдⷭ҇н.

Дїа́конъ: Хрⷭ҇тїа́нскїѧ кончи́ны живота̀ на́шегѡ, безболѣ́зненны, непосты́дны, ми́рны, и҆ до́брагѡ ѿвѣ́та на стра́шнѣмъ сꙋди́щи хрⷭ҇то́вѣ про́симъ.

Ли́къ: Пода́й, гдⷭ҇н.

Дїа́конъ: Прест҃ꙋ́ю, пречтⷭ҇ꙋ́ю, преблгⷭ҇ове́н_нꙋ́ю, сла́внꙋю влⷣчцꙋ на́шꙋ бцⷣꙋ, и҆ приснодв҃ꙋ мр҃і́ю со всѣ́ми ст҃ы́ми помѧнꙋ́вше, са́ми

Choir: Grant this, O Lord.

Deacon: An angel of peace, a faithful guide, a guardian of our souls and bodies, let us ask of the Lord.

Choir: Grant this, O Lord.

Deacon: Pardon and remission of our sins and offenses, let us ask of the Lord.

Choir: Grant this, O Lord.

Deacon: Things good and profitable for our souls, and peace for the world, let us ask of the Lord.

Choir: Grant this, O Lord.

Deacon: That we may complete the remaining time of our life in peace and repentance, let us ask of the Lord.

Choir: Grant this, O Lord.

Deacon: A Christian ending to our life, painless, blameless, peaceful, and a good defense before the dread judgment seat of Christ, let us ask.

Choir: Grant this, O Lord.

Deacon: Calling to remembrance our most holy, most pure, most blessed, glorious Lady

себѣ̀, и҆ дрꙋ́гъ дрꙋ́га, и҆ ве́сь живо́тъ на́шъ хрⷭ҇тꙋ̀ бг҃ꙋ предади́мъ.

Ли́къ: Тебѣ̀, гдⷭ҇и.

Возглаше́нїе: Ще́дротами є҆диноро́днагѡ сн҃а твоегѡ̀, съ ни́мже бл҃гослове́нъ є҆сѝ, со прест҃ы́мъ и҆ бл҃ги́мъ и҆ животворѧ́щимъ твои́мъ дх҃омъ, ны́нѣ и҆ при́снѡ, и҆ во вѣ́ки вѣкѡ́въ.

Ли́къ: А҆ми́нь.

Їере́й: Ми́ръ всѣ́мъ.

Ли́къ: И҆ дꙋ́хови твоемꙋ̀.

Дїа́конъ: Возлю́бимъ дрꙋ́гъ дрꙋ́га, да є҆диномы́слїемъ и҆сповѣ́мы.

Ли́къ: Оц҃а̀, и҆ сн҃а, и҆ ст҃а́гѡ дх҃а, трⷪ҇цꙋ є҆диносꙋ́щнꙋю, и҆ неразлѣ́льнꙋю.

И҆ сщ҃е́нникъ покланѧ́ется три́жды, глаго́лѧ та́йнѡ:

Возлюблю̀ тѧ̀, гдⷭ҇и, крѣ́посте моѧ̀, гдⷭ҇ь ᲂу҆твержде́нїе моѐ, и҆ прибѣ́жище моѐ, три́жды.

Theotokos and Ever-Virgin Mary, with all
the Saints, let us commit ourselves and one
another and all our life unto Christ, our God.

Choir: To Thee, O Lord.

Exclamation: Through the compassions
of Thine Only-begotten Son, with Whom
Thou art blessed, together with Thine all-
holy and good and life-creating Spirit, now
and ever, and unto the ages of ages.

Choir: Amen.

Priest: Peace be unto all.

Choir: And to thy spirit.

Deacon: Let us love one another, that with
one mind we may confess:

Choir: The Father, and the Son, and the Holy
Spirit: the Trinity one in essence and indivisible.

And the priest bows thrice, saying secretly:

I will love Thee, O Lord, my strength. The
Lord is my firm foundation, and my fortress
(thrice).

И҆ цѣлꙋетъ ст҃а́ѧ си́це, ꙗ҆́коже сꙋ́ть
покровены̀, пе́рвѣе верхꙋ̀ ст҃а́гѡ ді́скоса:
та́же верхꙋ̀ ст҃а́гѡ потира, и҆ кра́й ст҃ы́ѧ
трапе́зы пред̾ собою̀. А҆́ще ли бꙋ́дꙋтъ
сщ҃е́нникѡвъ два̀, и҆ли мно́жае, то и҆ ѻ҆нѝ
цѣлꙋ́ютъ ст҃а́ѧ всѝ, и҆ дрꙋ́гъ дрꙋ́га въ
ра́мена.

Настоѧ́тель же глаго́летъ:

Хрⷭ҇то́съ посредѣ̀ на́съ.

И҆ ѿвѣща́етъ цѣлова́вый:

И҆ є҆́сть, и҆ бꙋ́детъ.

Та́кожде и҆ дїа́кони, а҆́ще бꙋ́дꙋтъ два̀, и҆лѝ
трѝ, цѣлꙋ́ютъ кі́йждо ѻ҆ра́рь сво́й и҆дѣ́же
крⷭ҇та̀ ѻ҆́бразъ, и҆ дрꙋ́гъ дрꙋ́га въ ра́мена,
то́жде глаго́люще, ꙗ҆́же и҆ сщ҃е́нницы.

Подо́бнѣ же и҆ дїа́конъ спокланѧ́етсѧ, на
не́мже стои́тъ мѣ́стѣ, и҆ цѣлꙋетъ ѻ҆ра́рь
сво́й, и҆дѣ́же є҆́сть крⷭ҇та̀ ѻ҆́бразъ, и҆ та́кѡ
возглаша́етъ:

And he kisses the Holy Things that are covered, thus: first the top of the holy diskos, then the rim of the holy chalice and the edge of the Holy Table before him. If there be two priests, or more, then they all kiss the holy things, and one another on the shoulders.

The senior celebrant says:

Christ is in our midst.

And he that kisses replies:

He is, and shall be.

Likewise the deacons, if there be two, or three, kiss each his own orarion, where the figure of the Cross is, and one another on the shoulders, saying that which the priests have said.

In like manner the deacon bows, on the place where he stands, and kisses his orarion where the figure of the Cross is, and then exclaims:

Две́ри, две́ри, премꙋ́дростїю во́нмемъ.

Сщ҃е́нникъ же воздвиза́етъ воздꙋ́хъ, и҆ держи́тъ над̾ ст҃ы́ми дарми̂. А҆́ще же и҆ні́и бꙋ́дꙋтъ сщ҃е́нницы слꙋжа́щїи, та́кожде воздвиза́ютъ ст҃ы́й воздꙋ́хъ, и҆ держа́тъ над̾ ст҃ы́ми дарми̂, потрѧса́юще, и҆ глаго́люще въ себѣ̀, ꙗ҆́коже и҆ лю́дїе, и҆сповѣ́данїе вѣ́ры:

Вѣ́рꙋю во є҆ди́наго бг҃а ѻ҆ц҃а̀ вседержи́телѧ, творца̀ нб҃ꙋ̀ и҆ землѝ, ви́димымъ же всѣ̑мъ и҆ неви́димымъ. И҆ во є҆ди́наго гд҃а і҆и҃са хрⷭ҇та̀, сн҃а бж҃їѧ, є҆диноро́днаго, и҆́же ѿ ѻ҆ц҃а̀ рожде́ннаго пре́жде всѣ́хъ вѣ̑къ: свѣ́та ѿ свѣ́та, бг҃а и҆́стинна ѿ бг҃а и҆́стинна, рожде́нна, не сотворе́нна, є҆диносꙋ́щна ѻ҆ц҃ꙋ̀, и҆́мже всѧ̑ бы́ша. На́съ ра́ди человѣ́къ, и҆ на́шегѡ ра́ди сп҃се́нїѧ, сше́дшаго съ нб҃съ, и҆ воплоти́вшагосѧ ѿ дх҃а ст҃а и҆ мр҃і́и дв҃ы, и҆ вочл҃вѣ́чшасѧ. Распѧ́таго же за ны̀ при понті́йстѣмъ пїла́тѣ, и҆ страда́вша, и҆ погребе́нна, и҆ воскр҃ша́го въ тре́тїй де́нь по писа́нїємъ. И҆ возше́дшаго на нб҃са̀, и҆ сѣдѧ́ща ѡ҆деснꙋ́ю ѻ҆ц҃а̀. И҆ па́ки градꙋ́щаго

The doors, the doors! In wisdom let us attend.

The priest lifts up the aer, and holds it over the Holy Gifts. If there be other priests concelebrating, they likewise lift up the holy aer, and hold it over the Holy Gifts, waving it and saying secretly, as do the people also, the Confession of faith:

I believe in one God, the Father Almighty, Maker of heaven and earth and all things visible and invisible; and in one Lord Jesus Christ, the Son of God, the Only-begotten, begotten of the Father before all ages, Light of Light, true God of true God, begotten, not made, of one essence with the Father, by Whom all things were made; Who for us men and for our salvation came down from the Heavens, and was incarnate of the Holy Spirit and the Virgin Mary, and became man; and was crucified for us under Pontius Pilate, and suffered, and was buried; and arose on the third day according to the

со сла́вою, сꙋди́ти живы̑мъ и҆ ме́ртвымъ, е҆гѡ́же црⷭ҇твїю не бꙋ́детъ конца̀. И҆ въ дх҃а ст҃а́го, гдⷭ҇а, животворѧ́щаго, и҆́же ѿ ѻ҆ц҃а̀ и҆сходѧ́щаго, и҆́же со ѻ҆ц҃е́мъ и҆ сн҃омъ спокланѧ́ема и҆ сславима, глаго́лавшаго прⷪ҇ро́ки. Во е҆ди́нꙋ ст҃ꙋ́ю соборнꙋ́ю и҆ а҆пⷭ҇льскꙋ́ю цр҃ковь. И҆сповѣ́дꙋю е҆ди́но крⷭ҇ще́нїе во ѡ҆ставле́нїе грѣхѡ́въ. Ча́ю воскрⷭ҇нїѧ ме́ртвыхъ: И҆ жи́зни бꙋ́дꙋщагѡ вѣ́ка. А҆ми́нь.

Дїа́конъ: Ста́немъ добрѣ̀, ста́немъ со стра́хомъ, во́нмемъ, ст҃о́е возноше́нїе въ ми́рѣ приноси́ти.

Ли́къ: Ми́лость ми́ра, же́ртвꙋ хвале́нїѧ.

И҆ сщ҃е́нникъ ѹ҆́бѡ взе́мъ воздꙋ́хъ ѿ ст҃ы́хъ, и҆ цѣлова́въ и҆̀, полага́етъ на е҆ди́но мѣ́сто, глаго́лѧ:

Блгⷣть гдⷭ҇а на́шегѡ і҆и҃са хрⷭ҇та̀, и҆ любы̀

Scriptures; and ascended into the heavens, and sitteth at the right hand of the Father; and shall come again, with glory, to judge both the living and the dead, Whose kingdom shall have no end. And in the Holy Spirit, the Lord, the Giver of Life, Who proceedeth from the Father, Who with the Father and the Son together is worshipped and glorified, Who spake by the prophets. In One Holy, Catholic and Apostolic Church. I confess one baptism for the remission of sins. I look for the resurrection of the dead; and the life of the age to come. Amen.

Deacon: Let us stand well. Let us stand with fear. Let us attend, that we may offer the holy oblation in peace.

Choir: A mercy of peace, a sacrifice of praise.

The priest then having taken the aer off the Holy Gifts, and kissing it, lays it to one side, saying:

The grace of our Lord Jesus Christ, and the

бга и ѻ҆ц҃а, и҆ причасті́е ст҃а́гѡ дх҃а, бꙋ́ди со
всѣ́ми ва́ми.

Дїа́конъ же поклони́всѧ, вхо́дитъ во
ст҃ы́й ѻ҆лта́рь. И҆ прїи́мъ рꙗпі́дꙋ, вѣ́етъ
ст҃а̑ѧ бл҃гоговѣ́йнѡ. А҆́ще же нѣ́сть рꙗпі́ды,
твори́тъ сїѐ со є҆ди́нѣмъ покро́вцемъ.

Ли́къ: И҆ со дꙋ́хомъ твои́мъ.

Сщ҃е́нникъ: Горѣ̀ и҆мѣ́имъ сердца̀.

Ли́къ: И҆мамы ко гдꙋ̀.

Сщ҃е́нникъ: Бл҃годари́мъ гдⷭ҇а.

Ли́къ: Досто́йно и҆ пра́ведно єⷭ҇ть, покланѧ́тисѧ
ѻ҆ц҃ꙋ, и҆ сн҃ꙋ, и҆ ст҃о́мꙋ дх҃ꙋ, трⷪ҇цѣ є҆диносꙋ́щнѣй
и҆ нераздѣ́льнѣй.

Сщ҃е́нникъ же мо́литсѧ:

Досто́йно и҆ пра́ведно тѧ̀ пѣ́ти,
тѧ̀ бл҃гослови́ти, тѧ̀ хвали́ти, тѧ̀
бл҃годари́ти, тебѣ̀ покланѧ́тисѧ на
всѧ́комъ мѣ́стѣ вл҃чествїѧ твоегѡ̀: ты̀
бо є҆сѝ бг҃ъ неизрече́ненъ, недовѣ́домь,
неви́димь, непостижи́мь, при́снѡ сы́й,
та́кожде сы́й, ты̀ и҆ є҆диноро́дный тво́й

love of God the Father, and the communion of the Holy Spirit be with you all.

And the deacon, having bowed, enters the holy altar, and taking a fan, fans the Holy Things reverently. If there be no fan, he uses one of the veils.

Choir: And with thy spirit.

Priest: Let us lift up our hearts.

Choir: We lift them up unto the Lord.

Priest: Let us give thanks unto the Lord.

Choir: It is meet and right to worship the Father, the Son, and the Holy Spirit, the Trinity one in essence and indivisible.

The priest prays:

It is meet and right to hymn Thee, to bless Thee, to praise Thee, to give thanks unto Thee, to worship Thee in every place of Thy dominion, for Thou art God ineffable, incomprehensible, invisible, inconceivable, everexisting, eternally the same, Thou and Thine Only-begotten Son and Thy Holy Spirit.

сихъ, и дꙋхъ твой стый: ты ѿ небытїѧ
въ бытїе насъ привелъ еси, и ѿпадшыѧ
возставилъ еси паки, и не ѿстꙋпилъ еси
всѧ творѧ, дондеже насъ на нбо возвелъ
еси, и црство твое даровалъ еси бꙋдꙋщее. Ѡ
сихъ всѣхъ блгодаримъ тѧ, и единороднаго
твоегѡ сна, и дꙋха твоегѡ стагѡ, ѡ всѣхъ,
ихже вѣмы, и ихже не вѣмы, ꙗвленныхъ
и неꙗвленныхъ блгодѣѧнїихъ бывшихъ
на насъ. Блгодаримъ тѧ и ѡ слꙋжбѣ сей,
юже ѿ рꙋкъ нашихъ прїѧти изволилъ
еси, аще и предстоѧтъ тебѣ тысѧцы
архагглѡвъ, и тмы агглѡвъ, херꙋвїми и
серафїми, шестокрилатїи, многоочитїи,
возвышающїисѧ пернатїи.

Возглашенїе: Побѣднꙋю пѣснь поюще,
вопїюще, взывающе и глаголюще.

Ликъ: Стъ, стъ, стъ гдь саваѡѳъ, исполнь нбо
и землѧ славы твоеѧ, ѡсанна въ вышнихъ,

Thou didst call us from non-existence into being, and when we had fallen away, Thou didst raise us up again, and didst not cease to do all things until Thou hadst brought us up to heaven, and hadst bestowed upon us Thy kingdom which is to come. For all these things we give thanks unto Thee, and to Thine Only-begotten Son, and to Thy Holy Spirit, for all the things we know, and whereof we know not, for the benefits both manifest and hidden which have come upon us. We give thanks unto Thee also for this liturgy which Thou hast been pleased to accept from our hands, though there stand before Thee thousands of archangels and ten thousands of angels, the cherubim and seraphim, six-winged, many-eyed, borne aloft on their wings.

Exclamation: Singing the triumphal hymn, shouting, crying aloud, and saying:

Choir: Holy, Holy, Holy, Lord of Sabbaoth, heaven and earth are full of Thy glory.

Блгослове́нъ гряды́й во и҆́мѧ гдⷵне, ѡ҆са́нна въ вы́шнихъ.

И҆ здѣ̀ па́ки дїа́конъ, прїи́мъ ст҃ꙋю ѕвѣ́здицꙋ ѿ ст҃а́гѡ ді́скоса, твори́тъ крⷵта̀ ѻ҆́бразъ верхꙋ̀ є҆гѡ̀, и҆ цѣлова́въ ю҆̀, полага́етъ.

Та́же прихо́дитъ, и҆ ста́нетъ на десне́й странѣ̀: и҆ взе́мъ рїпі́дꙋ въ рꙋцѣ̀, ѡ҆ма́хиваетъ ти́хѡ со всѧ́кимъ внима́нїемъ и҆ стра́хомъ верхꙋ̀ ст҃ы́хъ дарѡ́въ, ꙗ҆́кѡ не сѣ́сти мꙋ́хамъ, ни и҆но́мꙋ чесомꙋ̀ таково́мꙋ.

Сщ҃е́нникъ мо́лится:

Съ си́ми и҆ мы̀ бл҃же́нными си́лами, влⷣко чл҃вѣколю́бче, вопїе́мъ и҆ глаго́лемъ: ст҃ъ є҆сѝ и҆ прест҃ъ, ты̀ и҆ є҆диноро́дный тво́й сн҃ъ, и҆ дх҃ъ тво́й ст҃ы́й. ст҃ъ є҆сѝ и҆ прест҃ъ, и҆ великолѣ́пна сла́ва твоѧ̀, и҆́же мі́ръ тво́й та́кѡ возлюби́лъ є҆сѝ, ꙗ҆́коже сн҃а твоегѡ̀ є҆диноро́днаго да́ти: да всѧ́къ вѣ́рꙋѧй въ него̀ не поги́бнетъ, но и҆́мать живо́тъ вѣ́чный: и҆́же прише́дъ, и҆ всѐ є҆́же ѡ҆ на́съ

Hosanna in the highest. Blessed is He that cometh in the Name of the Lord. Hosanna in the highest.

And here the deacon, taking the holy star from the holy diskos, makes the sign of the Cross above it, and kissing it, lays it aside.

Then the deacon goes and stands on the right side, and having taken a fan in his right hand, fans gently, with all attentiveness and fear, over the Holy Gifts, lest flies or other such insects settle on them.

The priest prays:

With these blessed hosts, O Master, Lover of mankind, we also cry aloud and say: Holy art Thou and most-holy, Thou, and Thine Only-begotten Son, and Thy Holy Spirit; holy art Thou and most-holy, and majestic is Thy glory, Who so loved Thy world that Thou gavest Thine Only-begotten Son, that whosoever believeth in Him should not perish, but have everlasting life,

смотрѣ́нїе и҆спо́лнивъ, въ но́щь въ ню́же предаѧ́шесѧ, па́че же са́мъ себѐ предаѧ́ше, за мі́рскі́й живо́тъ, прїе́мъ хлѣ́бъ во ст҃ы́ѧ своѧ̀, и҆ пречⷭ҇ты́ѧ и҆ непоро́чныѧ рꙋ́ки, бл҃годари́въ и҆ бл҃гослови́въ, ѡ҆ст҃и́въ, преломи́въ, даде́ ст҃ы́мъ свои́мъ ᲂу҆чн҃кѡ́мъ и҆ а҆плⷭ҇ѡмъ, ре́къ:

Возглаше́нїе: Прїими́те, ꙗ҆ди́те, сїѐ є҆́сть тѣ́ло моѐ, є҆́же за вы̀ ломи́мое во ѡ҆ставле́нїе грѣхѡ́въ.

Ли́къ: А҆ми́нь.

Сем́ꙋ же глаго́лемꙋ, показꙋ́етъ сщ҃е́нникꙋ дїа́конъ ст҃ы́й ді́скосъ, держа̀ и҆ ѻ҆ра́рь треми́ пе́рсты десни́цы. Подо́бнѣ, и҆ є҆гда̀ глаго́летъ сщ҃е́нникъ: Пі́йте ѿ неѧ̀ всѝ: споказꙋ́етъ и҆ са́мъ ст҃ы́й поти́рь.

Сщ҃е́нникъ та́йнѡ:

Подо́бнѣ и҆ ча́шꙋ по ве́чери, глаго́лѧ:

Возглаше́нїе: Пі́йте ѿ неѧ̀ всѝ, сїѧ̀ є҆́сть кро́вь моѧ̀ но́вагѡ завѣ́та, ꙗ҆́же за вы̀

Who, when He had come and fulfilled all the dispensation for us, on the night in which He was given up, or rather gave Himself up for the life of the world, took bread in His holy and most pure and unblemished hands, and when He had given thanks, and had blessed it, and hallowed it, and broken it, He gave it to His holy disciples and apostles, saying:

Exclamation: Take, eat: this is My Body, which is broken for you for the remission of sins.

Choir: Amen.

When this is being said, the deacon points to the holy diskos, holding his orarion with three fingers of his right hand. Likewise, when the priest says: Drink of it, all of you, he points to the holy chalice.

The priest prays secretly:

And likewise the cup after supper, saying: Exclamation: Drink of it, all of you: This is My Blood of the New Testament, which is

и҆ за мнѡ́гїѧ и҆зливае́маѧ, во ѡ҆ставле́нїе
грѣхѡ́въ.

Ли́къ: А҆ми́нь.

Сщ҃е́нникъ мо́литсѧ:

По́мина́юще ѹ҆́бѡ спаси́тельнꙋ́ю сїю̀
за́повѣдь, и҆ всѧ̑ ꙗ҆̀же ѡ҆ на́съ бы́вшаѧ:
крⷭ҇тъ, гро́бъ, трїдне́вное воскрⷭ҇нїе, на нб҃са̀
восхожде́нїе, ѡ҆деснꙋ́ю сѣдѣ́нїе, второ́е и҆
сла́вное па́ки прише́ствїе.

Возглаше́нїе: Твоѧ̑ ѿ твои́хъ тебѣ̀
принося́ще, ѡ҆ всѣ́хъ и҆ за всѧ̑.

Семꙋ̀ же глаго́лемꙋ, дїа́конъ
ѿлага́етъ рїпі́дꙋ, и҆ прело́жъ рꙋ́цѣ
крⷭ҇тоѡбра́знѣ, и҆ подъе́мъ ст҃ы́й
дї́скосъ, и҆ ст҃ы́й поти́ръ, и҆ поклони́тсѧ
ѹ҆миле́ннѣ.

Ли́къ: Тебѣ̀ пое́мъ, тебѣ̀ блгⷭ҇ови́мъ, тебѣ̀
блгⷣри́мъ гдⷭ҇и, и҆ мо́лимъ ти сѧ, бж҃е на́шъ.

shed for you and for many, for the remission of sins.

Choir: Amen.

The priest prays secretly:

Having called to remembrance, therefore, this saving commandment and all those things which came to pass for us: the Cross, the grave, the resurrection on the third day, the ascension into the heavens, the sitting at the right hand, the second and glorious coming again:

Exclamation: Thine Own of Thine Own, we offer unto Thee in behalf of all, and for all.

While this is being said, the deacon puts aside the fan, and having formed a cross with his arms, and having lifted the holy diskos and the holy chalice, he bows with compunction.

Choir: We praise Thee, we bless Thee, we give thanks unto Thee, O Lord, and we pray unto Thee, O our God.

Сщ҃е́нникъ же мо́литсѧ:

Е҆щѐ прино́симъ тѝ слове́снꙋю сі́ю и҆ безкро́внꙋю слꙋ́жбꙋ, и҆ про́симъ, и҆ мо́лимъ, и҆ ми́ли сѧ дѣ́емъ, низпослѝ дх҃а твоегѡ̀ ст҃а́го на ны̀, и҆ на предлежа́щыѧ да́ры сїѧ̑.

И҆ дїа́конъ прихо́дитъ бли́зъ ко і҆ере́ю, и҆ покланѧ́ютсѧ ѻ҆́ба три́жды пред ст҃о́ю трапе́зою, молѧ́щесѧ въ себѣ̀ и҆ глаго́люще:

Сщ҃е́нникъ: Гдⷭ҇и, и҆́же прест҃а́го твоегѡ̀ дх҃а въ тре́тїй ча́съ а҆пⷭ҇лѡмъ твои́мъ низпосла́вый, тогѡ̀, бл҃гі́й, не ѿими́ ѿ на́съ: но ѡ҆бновѝ на́съ молѧ́щихъ тѝ сѧ.

Дїа́конъ стіⷯ: Се́рдце чи́сто созижди во мнѣ̀, бж҃е, и҆ дх҃ъ пра́въ ѡ҆бновѝ во ᲂу҆тро́бѣ мое́й.

Па́ки сщ҃е́нникъ: Гдⷭ҇и, и҆́же прест҃а́го твоегѡ̀ дх҃а:

Дїа́конъ стіⷯ: Не ѿве́ржи менѐ ѿ лица̀ твоегѡ̀, и҆ дх҃а твоегѡ̀ ст҃а́гѡ не ѿими́ ѿ менѐ.

The priest prays secretly:

Again we offer unto Thee this rational and bloodless service, and we ask of Thee, and we pray Thee, and we entreat Thee: Send down Thy Holy Spirit upon us and upon these Gifts set forth.

And the deacon draws nigh to the priest, and both of them bow thrice before the Holy Table, praying secretly and saying:

Priest: O Lord, Who didst send down Thy Most holy Spirit at the third hour upon Thine apostles: Take Him not from us, O Good One, but renew Him in us who pray unto Thee.

Deacon, the verse: Create in me a clean heart, O God, and renew a right spirit within me.

Again, the priest: O Lord, Who didst send down Thy Most-holy Spirit . . .

Deacon, the verse: Cast me not away from Thy presence, and take not Thy Holy Spirit from me.

Й па́ки сщⷵе́нникъ: Гдⷭ҇и, и҆́же престтⷢ҇а́го
твоегѡ̀ дх҃а:

Та́же главꙋ̀ подклони́въ дїа́конъ, и҆ показꙋ́ѧ
со ѻ҆раре́мъ стⷤ҃ый хлⷭ҇ѣ́бъ, глаго́летъ та́йнѡ:

Блⷭ҇гослови́, влады́ко, стⷤ҃ый хлⷭ҇ѣ́бъ.

Сщⷵе́нникъ же воста́въ, зна́менꙋетъ ст҃ы̑ѧ
да́ры, глаго́ла:

Й сотворѝ ᲂу҆́бѡ хлⷭ҇ѣ́бъ се́й чⷭ҇тно́е тⷮѣ́ло
хрⷭ҇та̀ твоегѡ̀.

Дїа́конъ: А҆ми́нь.

Й па́ки дїа́конъ:

Блⷭ҇гослови́, влады́ко, стⷤ҃ю ча́шꙋ.

Й сщⷵе́нникъ блⷭ҇гословлѧ́ѧ глаго́летъ:

А҆ є҆́же въ ча́ши се́й, чⷭ҇тнꙋ́ю кро́вь хрⷭ҇та̀
твоегѡ̀.

Дїа́конъ: А҆ми́нь.

Й па́ки дїа́конъ, показꙋ́ѧ и҆ ѻ҆боѧ̀ ст҃а̑ѧ,
глаго́летъ:

And again, the priest: **O Lord, Who didst send down Thy Most-holy Spirit . . .**

Then bowing his head and pointing with his orarion to the Holy Bread, the deacon says quietly:

Bless, master, the Holy Bread.

And the priest, rising, makes the sign of the Cross over the Holy Bread:

And make this Bread the precious Body of Thy Christ.
Deacon: **Amen.**

And again, the deacon:

Bless, master, the Holy Cup.

And the priest, blessing, says:

And that which is in this Cup, the precious Blood of Thy Christ.
Deacon: **Amen.**

And again the deacon, pointing to both the Holy Things, says:

Бл҃гословѝ, влады́ко, ѻ҆боѧ̀.

Сщ҃е́нникъ же, бл҃гословлѧ́ѧ ѻ҆боѧ̀ ст҃а̑ѧ,
глаго́летъ:

Преложи́въ дх҃омъ твои́мъ ст҃ы́мъ.
Дїа́конъ: А҆ми́нь, а҆ми́нь, а҆ми́нь.

И҆ главꙋ̀ подклони́въ дїа́конъ сщ҃е́нникꙋ, и҆
ре́къ:

Помѧни́ мѧ, ст҃ы́й влады́ко, грѣ́шнаго.
Сщ҃е́нникъ же глаго́летъ: Да помѧне́тъ тѧ̀
гдⷭ҇ь бг҃ъ во црⷭ҇твїи свое́мъ всегда̀, ны́нѣ и҆
при́снѡ, и҆ во вѣ́ки вѣкѡ́въ.
Дїа́конъ же ре́къ: А҆ми́нь, преходи́тъ, на
не́мже пе́рвѣе стоѧ́ше мѣ́стѣ, и҆ взе́мъ
рїпїдꙋ̀, ѡ҆ма́хиваетъ ст҃а̑ѧ ꙗ҆́кѡ и҆ пре́жде.

Сщ҃е́нникъ же мо́литсѧ:

Ꙗ҆́коже бы́ти причаща́ющымсѧ во
трезвѣ́нїе дꙋшѝ, во ѡ҆ставле́нїе
грѣхѡ́въ, въ прїѡбще́нїе ст҃а́гѡ твоегѡ̀
дх҃а, во и҆сполне́нїе црⷭ҇твїѧ нбⷭ҇нагѡ, въ

Bless them both, master.

And the priest, blessing both the Holy
Things, says:

Changing them by Thy Holy Spirit.
Deacon: Amen, amen, amen.

And the deacon, bowing his head to the
priest, says:

Remember me, a sinner, holy master.
And the priest says: May the Lord God
remember thee in His kingdom, always,
now and ever, and unto the ages of ages.
And the deacon says: Amen, and goes to the
place where he first stood, and taking a fan,
fans the Holy Things as before.

And the priest prays:

That to them that shall partake thereof,
they may be unto sobriety of soul, unto
remission of sins, unto the communion of
Thy Holy Spirit, unto the fullness of the

дерзновéнїе є҆́же къ тебѣ̀, не въ сꙋ́дъ, и҆лѝ во ѡ҆сꙋждéнїе.

Є҆щѐ прино́симъ тѝ словéснꙋю сїю̀ слꙋ́жбꙋ, ѡ҆ и҆́же въ вѣ́рѣ почи́вшихъ, прао́тцѣхъ, ѻ҆тцѣ́хъ, патрїа́рсѣхъ, прⷬ҇ро́цѣхъ, а҆пⷭ҇лѣхъ, проповѣ́дницѣхъ, є҆ѵⷢ҇лі́стѣхъ, мⷱ҇ницѣ́хъ, и҆сповѣ́дницѣхъ, воздéржницѣхъ, и҆ ѡ҆ всѧ́комъ дꙋ́сѣ прáведнѣмъ въ вѣ́рѣ скончáвшемсѧ.

И҆ прїéмъ кади́ло, сщ҃éнникъ возглашáетъ:

И҆зрѧ́днѡ ѡ҆ престѣ́й, пречⷭ҇тѣ́й, преблⷭ҇гословéннѣй, слáвнѣй влⷣчцѣ нáшей бцⷣѣ и҆ приснодв҃ѣ мр҃і́и.

И҆ кади́тъ пред̾ ст҃óю трапéзою три́жды. Тáже дїáконъ кади́тъ ст҃ꙋ́ю трапéзꙋ ѻ҆́крестъ, и҆ поминáетъ ꙗ҆́же хо́щетъ живы́ѧ и҆ мéртвыѧ.

Ли́къ поéтъ: Досто́йно є҆́сть ꙗ҆́кѡ вои́стиннꙋ, блж҃и́ти тѧ̀ бцⷣꙋ, присноблж҃éннꙋю, и҆ пренепоро́чнꙋю, и҆ мт҃рь бг҃а нáшегѡ.

kingdom of heaven, unto boldness toward Thee, not unto judgment or condemnation.

Again we offer unto Thee this rational service for them that in faith have gone to their rest before us: the forefathers, fathers, patriarchs, prophets, apostles, preachers, evangelists, martyrs, confessors, ascetics, and for every righteous spirit made perfect in faith.

And taking the censer, the priest exclaims:

Especially for our most holy, most pure, most blessed, glorious Lady Theotokos and Ever-Virgin Mary.

And he censes before the Holy Table thrice. Likewise, the deacon censes the Holy Table round about, and commemorates the living and the departed, whomever he wishes.

The choir chants: It is truly meet to bless thee, the Theotokos, ever-blessed and most-blameless, and Mother of our God. More

Чⷮнѣ́йшꙋю херꙋві́мъ, и҆ сла́внѣйшꙋю безⸯ
сравне́нїѧ серафі́мъ, безⸯ и҆стлѣ́нїѧ бг҃а сло́ва
ро́ждшꙋю, сꙋ́щꙋю бц҃ꙋ тѧ̀ велича́емъ.

Дїа́конъ помина́етъ дїптѵ́ха, си́рѣчь,
пома́нникъ ᲂу҆со́пшихъ.

Сщ҃е́нникъ же мо́литсѧ: Ѡ҆ ст҃е́мъ і҆ѡа́ннѣ
прⷪро́цѣ, прⷣте́чи и҆ крⷭти́тели, ѡ҆ ст҃ы́хъ
сла́вныхъ и҆ всехва́льныхъ а҆пⷭтоле́хъ,
ѡ҆ ст҃е́мъ и҆м҃къ, е҆гѡ́же и҆ па́мѧть
совершае́мъ, и҆ ѡ҆ всѣ́хъ ст҃ы́хъ твои́хъ:
и҆́хже моли́твами посѣти́ на́съ, бж҃е.

И҆ помѧнѝ всѣ́хъ ᲂу҆со́пшихъ ѡ҆ наде́жди
воскрⷭнїѧ жи́зни вѣ́чныѧ (и҆ помина́етъ,
и҆́хже хо́щетъ, ᲂу҆со́пшихъ по и҆менѡ́мъ),
и҆ ᲂу҆поко́й и҆́хъ, и҆дѣ́же присѣща́етъ свѣ́тъ
лица̀ твоегѡ̀.

Е҆щѐ мо́лимъ тѧ̀, помѧнѝ, гдⷭи,
вса́кое е҆пⷭкпство правосла́вныхъ, пра́вѡ
пра́вѧщихъ сло́во твоеѧ̀ и҆́стины, вса́кое

honorable than the Cherubim, and beyond compare more glorious than the Seraphim, who without corruption gavest birth to God the Word, the very Theotokos, thee do we magnify.

The deacon commemorates the names of the departed.

And the priest prays: For the holy Prophet, Forerunner, and Baptist John, for the holy and all-praised apostles; for Saint(s) N., whose memory we also celebrate, and for all Thy saints, through whose intercessions do Thou visit us, O God.

And remember all that have departed in the hope of the resurrection unto life everlasting (and he commemorates by name whomever he wishes from among the departed), and grant them rest where the light of Thy countenance shall visit them.

Again we pray Thee: remember, O Lord, all the Orthodox episcopate that rightly divide the word of Thy truth, all

пресвv́терство, во хрⷮт҇ѣ̀ дїа́конство, и҆
всѧ́кїй сщ҃е́нническїй чи́нъ.

Е҆щѐ прино́симъ тѝ словⷭ҇еꙋ́ю сїю̀
слꙋ́жбꙋ ѡ҆ вселе́ннѣй, ѡ҆ ст҃ѣй собо́рнѣй
и҆ а҆пⷭ҇льстѣй цр҃кви, ѡ҆ и҆́же въ чистотѣ̀ и҆
честнѣ́мъ жи́тельствѣ пребыва́ющихъ: ѡ҆
бг҃охрани́мѣй странѣ̀ рѡссі́йстѣй, ѡ҆ странѣ̀
се́й, власте́хъ и҆ во́инствѣ є҆ѧ̀. Да́ждь и҆̀мъ,
гдⷭ҇и, ми́рное правле́нїе, да и҆ мы̀ въ тишинѣ̀
и҆́хъ ти́хое и҆ безмо́лвное житїѐ поживе́мъ,
во всѧ́комъ бл҃гоче́стїи и҆ чистотѣ̀.

И҆ по пѣ́нїи стїха̀, сщ҃е́нникъ возглаша́етъ:

Въ пе́рвыхъ помѧнѝ, гдⷭ҇и, вели́каго
господи́на и҆ ѻ҆тца̀ на́шего и҆́мⷬ҇къ,
ст҃ѣ́йшаго патрїа́рха моско́вскаго и҆ всеѧ̀
рꙋ́си, и҆ господи́на на́шего высокопреш_
сщ҃е́ннѣйшаго и҆́мⷬ҇къ, митрополі́та
восто́чно_а҆мерика́нскаго и҆ нью_
їо́ркскаго, первоїера́рха рꙋ́сскїѧ зарꙋбѣ́_
жныѧ цр҃кве, и҆ господи́на на́шего,
высокопрешсщ҃е́ннѣйшаго и҆́мⷬ҇къ [и҆лѝ
прешсщ҃е́ннѣйшаго и҆́мⷬ҇къ], а҆рхїепⷭ҇кпа [и҆лѝ

the priesthood, the diaconate in Christ, and
every sacred rank.

Again we offer unto Thee this rational
service for the whole world, for the Holy,
Catholic, and Apostolic Church, for them
that abide in purity and an honorable life,
for the God-preserved Russian land, for
this land, its authorities and armed forces.
Grant them, O Lord, peaceful governance,
that in their calm we also may lead a quiet
and peaceful life in all piety and purity.

And after the chanting of the hymn, the
priest exclaims:

Among the first, remember, O Lord,
our great lord and father N., the Most
Holy Patriarch of Moscow and All Russia,
and our lord, the Very Most Reverend N.,
Metropolitan of Eastern America and New
York, First Hierarch of the Russian Church
Abroad, and our lord, the Most [or Right]
Reverend N., Archbishop [or Bishop] of
[his see is commemorated here], whom

є҆пⷭ҇кпа] [є҆гꙋ́же є҆́сть ѻ҆́бласть], и҆́хже да́рꙋй ст҃ы̑мъ твои̑мъ цр҃квамъ, въ ми́рѣ, цѣ́лыхъ, чⷭ҇тныхъ, здра́выхъ, долгоде́нствꙋющихъ, пра́вѡ пра́вѧщихъ сло́во твоеѧ̀ и҆́стины.

И҆ пѣвцы̀ пою́тъ: И҆ всѣ́хъ, и҆ всѧ̑.

Та́же и҆ дїа́конъ помина́етъ пома́нникъ живы́хъ.

Сщ҃е́нникъ же мо́литсѧ:

Помѧнѝ, гдⷭ҇и, гра́дъ се́й, въ не́мже живе́мъ [и҆лѝ ве́сь сїю̀, въ не́йже живе́мъ, и҆лѝ ѻ҆би́тель сїю̀, въ не́йже живе́мъ], и҆ всѧ́кїй гра́дъ и҆ странꙋ̀, и҆ вѣ́рою живꙋ́щихъ въ ни́хъ. Помѧнѝ, гдⷭ҇и, пла́вающихъ, пꙋтеше́ствꙋющихъ, недꙋ́гꙋющихъ, стра́ждꙋщихъ, плѣне́нныхъ, и҆ спⷭ҇е́нїе и҆́хъ. Помѧнѝ, гдⷭ҇и, плодоносѧ́щихъ и҆ добротворѧ́щихъ во ст҃ы́хъ твои́хъ цр҃квахъ, и҆ поминѧ́ющихъ оу҆бѡ́гїѧ, и҆ на всѧ̑ ны̀ ми́лѡсти твоѧ̑ низпослѝ.

Возглаше́нїе: И҆ да́ждь на́мъ є҆ди́нѣми оу҆сты̀ и҆ є҆ди́нѣмъ се́рдцемъ сла́вити и҆ воспѣва́ти пречⷭ҇тно́е и҆ великолѣ́пое и҆́мѧ

do Thou grant unto Thy holy churches in peace, safety, honor, health and length of days, rightly dividing the word of Thy truth.

Choir: And each and every one.

And the deacon commemorates the names of the living.

The priest prays:

Remember, O Lord, this city [or village, or monastery] wherein we dwell, and every city and country and the faithful that dwell therein. Remember, O Lord, them that travel by sea, land, and air, the sick, the suffering, the captives, and their salvation. Remember, O Lord, them that bear fruit and do good works in Thy holy churches, and them that are mindful of the poor, and upon us all send down Thy mercy.

Exclamation: And grant unto us that with one mouth and one heart we may glorify and hymn Thy most honorable and majestic name: of the Father, and of the Son, and of

твоѐ, ѻ҆ц҃а̀, и҆ сн҃а, и҆ ст҃а́гѡ дх҃а, ны́нѣ и҆ при́снѡ, и҆ во вѣ́ки вѣкѡ́въ.

Ли́къ: А҆ми́нь.

Сщ҃е́нникъ, ѡ҆бра́щьсѧ ко две́ремъ и҆ бл҃гословлѧ́ѧ, глаго́летъ:

И҆ да бꙋ́дꙋтъ ми́лѡсти вели́кагѡ бг҃а и҆ сп҃са на́шегѡ і҆и҃са хр҃та̀ со всѣ́ми ва́ми.

Ли́къ: И҆ со дꙋ́хомъ твои́мъ.

Дїа́конъ, прїе́мъ бл҃гослове́нїе ѿ сщ҃е́нника и҆ и҆зше́дъ, ста́въ на ѻ҆бы́чномъ мѣ́стѣ, глаго́летъ:

Всѧ̀ ст҃ы̑ѧ помѧнꙋ́вше, па́ки и҆ па́ки ми́ромъ гдꙋ̀ помо́лимсѧ.

Ли́къ: Гд҃и, поми́лꙋй.

Дїа́конъ: Ѡ҆ принесе́нныхъ и҆ ѡ҆сщ҃е́нныхъ чⷭ҇тны́хъ дарѣ́хъ, гдꙋ̀ помо́лимсѧ.

Ли́къ: Гд҃и, поми́лꙋй.

Дїа́конъ: Ꙗ҆́кѡ да чл҃вѣколю́бецъ бг҃ъ на́шъ, прїе́мъ ѧ҆̀ во ст҃ы́й и҆ пренбⷭ҇ный и҆ мы́сленный сво́й же́ртвенникъ, въ воню̀

the Holy Spirit, now and ever, and unto the ages of ages.

Choir: Amen.

The priest turns toward the doors and blesses, saying:

And may the mercies of our great God and Saviour Jesus Christ be with you all.

Choir: And with thy spirit.

The deacon, having received a blessing from the priest, goes out and, standing in the usual place, says:

Having called to remembrance all the Saints, again and again, in peace let us pray to the Lord.

Choir: Lord, have mercy.

Deacon: For the precious Gifts set forth and sanctified, let us pray to the Lord.

Choir: Lord, have mercy.

Deacon: That our God, the Lover of mankind, having accepted them upon His holy and noetic altar above the heavens as an

бл҃гоꙋха́нїѧ дꙋхо́внагѡ, возниспо́слетъ
на́мъ бж҃е́ственнꙋю блⷢ҇да́ть и да́ръ ст҃а́гѡ
дх҃а, помо́лимсѧ.

Ли́къ: Гдⷭ҇и, помилꙋй.

Дїа́конъ: Ѡ изба́витисѧ на́мъ ѿ всѧ́кїѧ
ско́рби, гнѣ́ва и нꙋ́жды, гдⷭ҇ꙋ помо́лимсѧ.

Ли́къ: Гдⷭ҇и, помилꙋй.

Сщ҃е́нникъ же мо́литсѧ:

Тебѣ̀ предлага́емъ живо́тъ на́шъ ве́сь
и наде́ждꙋ, влⷣко чл҃вѣколю́бче, и
про́симъ, и мо́лимъ, и ми́ли сѧ дѣ́емъ,
сподо́би на́съ причасти́тисѧ нбⷭ҇ныхъ
твои́хъ и стра́шныхъ та́инъ, сеѧ̀ сщ҃е́нныѧ
и дꙋхо́вныѧ трапе́зы, съ чи́стою со́вѣстїю,
во ѡставле́нїе грѣхѡ́въ, въ проще́нїе
согрѣше́нїй, во ѻбще́нїе дх҃а ст҃а́гѡ, въ
наслѣ́дїе црⷭ҇твїѧ нбⷭ҇нагѡ, въ дерзнове́нїе
ѩ́же къ тебѣ̀, не въ сꙋ́дъ или во ѡсꙋжде́нїе.

Дїа́конъ: Застꙋпѝ, спасѝ, помилꙋй и
сохранѝ на́съ, бж҃е, твое́ю блⷢ҇да́тїю.

odor of spiritual fragrance, will send down upon us divine grace and the gift of the Holy Spirit, let us pray.

Choir: Lord, have mercy.

Deacon: That we may be delivered from all tribulation, wrath, and necessity, let us pray to the Lord.

Choir: Lord, have mercy.

The priest prays:

Unto Thee we offer our whole life and hope, O Master, Lover of mankind, and we ask Thee, and pray Thee, and supplicate Thee: vouchsafe us to partake of Thy heavenly and dread Mysteries of this sacred and spiritual Table, with a pure conscience, unto remission of sins, unto pardon of offences, unto communion of Thy Holy Spirit, unto inheritance of the kingdom of heaven, unto boldness toward Thee; not unto judgment, nor unto condemnation.

Deacon: Help us, save us, have mercy on us, and keep us, O God, by Thy grace.

Ли́къ: Гд҃и, поми́лꙋй.

Дїа́конъ: Днѐ всегѡ̀ соверше́нна, ст҃а, ми́рна и҆ безгрѣ́шна, ᲂу҆ гд҃а про́симъ.

Ли́къ: Пода́й, гд҃и.

Дїа́конъ: А҆́гг҃ла ми́рна, вѣ́рна наста́вника, храни́телѧ дꙋ́шъ и҆ тѣле́съ на́шихъ, ᲂу҆ гд҃а про́симъ.

Ли́къ: Пода́й, гд҃и.

Дїа́конъ: Проще́нїѧ и҆ ѡ҆ставле́нїѧ грѣхѡ́въ и҆ прегрѣше́нїй на́шихъ, ᲂу҆ гд҃а про́симъ.

Ли́къ: Пода́й, гд҃и.

Дїа́конъ: До́брыхъ и҆ поле́зныхъ дꙋша́мъ на́шымъ, и҆ ми́ра мі́рови, ᲂу҆ гд҃а про́симъ.

Ли́къ: Пода́й, гд҃и.

Дїа́конъ: Про́чее вре́мѧ живота̀ на́шегѡ въ ми́рѣ и҆ покаѧ́нїи сконча́ти, ᲂу҆ гд҃а про́симъ.

Ли́къ: Пода́й, гд҃и.

Дїа́конъ: Хрⷭ҇тїа́нскїѧ кончи́ны живота̀ на́шегѡ, безболѣ́знены, непосты́дны,

Choir: Lord, have mercy.

Deacon: That the whole day may be perfect, holy, peaceful, and sinless, let us ask of the Lord.

Choir: Grant this, O Lord.

Deacon: An angel of peace, a faithful guide, a guardian of our souls and bodies, let us ask of the Lord.

Choir: Grant this, O Lord.

Deacon: Pardon and remission of our sins and offenses, let us ask of the Lord.

Choir: Grant this, O Lord.

Deacon: Things good and profitable for our souls, and peace for the world, let us ask of the Lord.

Choir: Grant this, O Lord.

Deacon: That we may complete the remaining time of our life in peace and repentance, let us ask of the Lord.

Choir: Grant this, O Lord.

Deacon: A Christian ending to our life, painless, blameless, peaceful, and a good defense

ми́рны и҆ до́браго ѿвѣ́та на стра́шнѣмъ
сꙋди́щи хрⷭ҇то́вѣ про́симъ.

Ли́къ: Пода́й, гдⷭ҇и.

Дїа́конъ: Соедине́нїе вѣ́ры, и҆ причꙋ́стїе ст҃а́гѡ
дх҃а и҆спроси́вше, са́ми себѐ, и҆ дрꙋ́гъ дрꙋ́га,
и҆ ве́сь живо́тъ на́шъ хрⷭ҇тꙋ̀ бг҃ꙋ предади́мъ.

Ли́къ: Тебѣ̀, гдⷭ҇и.

Сщ҃е́нникъ возглаше́нїе: И҆ сподо́би на́съ,
влⷣко, со дерзнове́нїемъ, неѡсꙋжде́ннѡ
смѣ́ти призыва́ти тебѐ нбⷭ҇наго бг҃а ѻ҆ц҃а̀,
и҆ глаго́лати.

Лю́дїе: Ѻ҆́ч҃е на́шъ, и҆́же є҆сѝ на нб҃сѣ́хъ, да
ст҃и́тсѧ и҆́мѧ твоѐ, да прїи́детъ црⷭ҇твїе твоѐ:
да бꙋ́детъ во́лѧ твоѧ̀, ꙗ҆́кѡ на нб҃сѝ, и҆ на
землѝ. Хлѣ́бъ на́шъ насꙋ́щный да́ждь на́мъ
дне́сь, и҆ ѡ҆ста́ви на́мъ до́лги на́ша, ꙗ҆́коже и҆
мы̀ ѡ҆ставлѧ́емъ должникѡ́мъ на́шымъ: и҆
не введѝ на́съ во и҆скꙋше́нїе, но и҆зба́ви на́съ
ѿ лꙋка́ваго.

Сщ҃е́нникъ: Ꙗ҆́кѡ твоѐ є҆́сть црⷭ҇тво, и҆ си́ла,
и҆ сла́ва, ѻ҆ц҃а̀, и҆ сн҃а, и҆ ст҃а́гѡ дх҃а, ны́нѣ и҆
при́снѡ, и҆ во вѣ́ки вѣкѡ́въ.

before the dread judgment seat of Christ, let us ask.

Choir: Grant this, O Lord.

Deacon: Having asked for the unity of the faith and the communion of the Holy Spirit, let us commit ourselves and one another and all our life unto Christ, our God.

Choir: To Thee, O Lord.

Exclamation: And vouchsafe us, O Master, that with boldness and without condemnation we may dare to call upon Thee, the heavenly God and Father, and to say:

People: Our Father, Who art in the heavens, hallowed be Thy Name. Thy Kingdom come, Thy will be done, on earth as it is in heaven. Give us this day our daily bread, and forgive us our debts, as we forgive our debtors; and lead us not into temptation, but deliver us from the evil one.

Priest: For Thine is the kingdom, and the power and the glory, of the Father, and of the Son, and of the Holy Spirit, now and ever, and unto the ages of ages.

Ли́къ: Ами́нь.

Сщ҃е́нникъ: Ми́ръ все́мъ.

Ли́къ: И҆ дꙋ́хови твоемꙋ̀.

Дїа́конъ: Главы̑ ва́шѧ гд҃еви приклони́те.

Ли́къ: Тебѣ̀, гд҃и.

Сщ҃е́нникъ же мо́литсѧ та́йнѡ:

Бл҃года́римъ тѧ̀, цр҃ю̀ неви́димый, и҆́же неисче́тною твое́ю си́лою всѧ̑ содѣ́тельствовалъ є҆сѝ, и҆ мно́жествомъ ми́лости твоеѧ̀ ѿ небытїѧ̀ въ бытїѐ всѧ̑ приве́лъ є҆сѝ: са́мъ, влⷣко, съ нб҃сѐ при́зри на подкло́ншыѧ тебѣ̀ главы̑ своѧ̑, не бо̀ подклони́ша пло́ти и҆ кро́ви, но тебѣ̀, стра́шномꙋ бг҃ꙋ. ты̀ оу҆́бо, влⷣко, предлежа́щаѧ все́мъ на́мъ во бл҃го́е и҆зравнѧ́й, по коегѡ́ждо свое́й потре́бѣ: пла́вающымъ сплавай, пꙋтеше́ствꙋющымъ спꙋтеше́ствꙋй, недꙋ́гꙋющыѧ и҆сцѣлѝ, врачꙋ̀ дꙋ́шъ и҆ тѣле́съ.

Choir: Amen.

Priest: **Peace be unto all.**

Choir: And to thy spirit.

Deacon: **Bow your heads unto the Lord.**

Choir: To Thee, O Lord.

And the priest prays secretly:

We give thanks unto Thee, O invisible King, Who by Thine immeasurable might hast created all things, and in the multitude of Thy mercies hast brought all things from non-existence into being; do Thou Thyself, O Master, look down from heaven upon them that have bowed their heads unto Thee, for they have not bowed down unto flesh and blood, but unto Thee, the awesome God. Do Thou, therefore, O Master, distribute these Things here set forth unto us all for good, according to the need of each: sail with them that voyage, journey with them that travel, heal the sick, O Physician of souls and bodies.

Возглаше́нїе: Благода́тїю, и҆ щедро́тами, и҆ чл҃вѣколю́бїемъ є҆диноро́днагѡ сн҃а твоегѡ̀, съ ни́мже бл҃гослове́нъ є҆сѝ, со прест҃ы́мъ и҆ бл҃ги́мъ и҆ животворѧ́щимъ твои́мъ дх҃омъ, ны́нѣ и҆ при́снѡ, и҆ во вѣ́ки вѣкѡ́въ.

Ли́къ: А҆ми́нь.

Сщ҃е́нникъ мо́литсѧ:

Вонмѝ, гд҃и і҆и҃се хрⷭ҇тѐ бж҃е на́шъ, ѿ ст҃а́гѡ жили́ща твоегѡ̀, и҆ ѿ прⷭ҇то́ла сла́вы црⷭ҇твїѧ твоегѡ̀, и҆ прїидѝ во є҆́же ѡ҆ст҃и́ти на́съ, и҆́же горѣ̀ со ѻ҆ц҃е́мъ сѣдѧ́й, и҆ здѣ̀ на́мъ неви́димѡ спребыва́ѧй: и҆ сподо́би держа́вною твое́ю рꙋко́ю препода́ти на́мъ пречⷭ҇тое тѣ́ло твоѐ и҆ чⷭ҇тнꙋ́ю кро́вь, и҆ на́ми всѣ́мъ лю́демъ.

Се́й моли́твѣ глаго́лемѣй, дїа́конъ стоѧ́й пред ст҃ы́ми две́рьми, ѡ҆поѧсꙋ́етсѧ ѻ҆раре́мъ крⷭ҇тови́днѡ.

Exclamation: Through the grace and compassions and love for mankind of Thine Only-begotten Son, with Whom Thou art blessed, together with Thy Most-holy and good and life-creating Spirit, now and ever, and unto the ages of ages.

Choir: Amen.

The priest prays:

Attend, O Lord Jesus Christ our God, out of Thy holy dwelling-place and from the glorious throne of Thy kingdom, and come and sanctify us, O Thou that sittest with the Father on high, and invisibly abidest here with us, and vouchsafe by Thy strong right hand to impart unto us Thy most pure Body and precious Blood, and through us to all the people.

While this prayer is being said, the deacon, standing before the holy doors, girds himself with his orarion in the shape of a cross.

Та́же покланѧ́етсѧ сщⷭ҇е́нникъ, подобнѣ̀
й дїа́конъ, на не́мже стои́тъ мѣ́стѣ,
глаго́люще та́йнѡ, три́жды: Бж҃е, ѡ҆чи́сти
мѧ̀ грѣ́шнаго й помилꙋ́й мѧ̀.

Е҆гда̀ же ви́дитъ дїа́конъ сщⷭ҇е́нника
простира́юща рꙋ́цѣ, й прикаса́ющаꙗсѧ
стⷪ҇мꙋ хлѣ́бꙋ, во є҆́же сотвори́ти ст҃о́е
возноше́нїе, возглаша́етъ:

Во́нмемъ.

Сщⷭ҇е́нникъ же, возносѧ̀ ст҃ы́й хлѣ́бъ,
возглаша́етъ:

Ст҃а̑ѧ ст҃ы̑мъ.

Ли́къ: Е҆ди́нъ ст҃ъ, є҆ди́нъ гдⷭ҇ь, і҆и҃съ хрⷭ҇то́съ, во
сла́вꙋ бг҃а ѻ҆ц҃а̀. А҆ми́нь.

Й пою́тъ ли́цы кїнѡнїкъ днѐ, йлѝ ст҃а́гѡ.

Дїа́конъ же вхо́дитъ во ст҃ы́й ѻ҆лта́рь, й
ста́въ ѡ҆десну́ю сщⷭ҇е́нника, держа́щагѡ ст҃ы́й
хлѣ́бъ, глаго́летъ:

Раздроби́, влады́ко, ст҃ы́й хлѣ́бъ.

Then the priest bows, and likewise the deacon, at the place where he stands, while saying, thrice: **O God, cleanse me, a sinner, and have mercy on me.**

And when the deacon sees the priest stretch out his hands and touch the Holy Bread in order to make the holy elevation, he exclaims:

Let us attend.

And the priest, elevating the Holy Bread, exclaims:

Holy Things are for the holy.
Choir: **One is holy, One is Lord, Jesus Christ, to the glory of God the Father. Amen.**

And the choirs chant the communion verse of the day, or of the Saint.

And the deacon goes into the holy altar, and standing at the right hand of the priest, says:

Break the Holy Bread, master.

Сщⷣе́нникъ же раздробла́я и҆ на четы́ре ча́сти со внима́нїемъ и҆ бл҃гоговѣ́нїемъ, глаго́летъ:

Раздробла́етсѧ и҆ разⷣѣла́етсѧ а҆́гнецъ бж҃їй, раздробла́емый и҆ неразⷣѣла́емый, всегда̀ ꙗ҆до́мый и҆ никогда́же и҆жⷣива́емый, но причаща́ющыѧсѧ ѡ҆сщⷣа́й.

Ѡ҆ раздроблнѣ́їи ст҃а́гѡ а҆́гнца.

Подоба́етъ тебѣ̀ вѣ́дати, ѡ҆ і҆ере́е, ꙗ҆́кѡ, раздробла́я ст҃ы́й а҆́гнецъ, полага́й ча́сти кр҃тнымъ зна́менїемъ до́лꙋ ко ст҃о́мꙋ ди́скосꙋ, закла́нїемъ же горѣ̀, ꙗ҆́коже пре́жⷣе е҆гда̀ закала́шесѧ. І҆Н҃С, оу҆́бѡ полага́й на

And the priest, breaking it into four parts with attentiveness and reverence, says:

Broken and distributed is the Lamb of God: broken, yet not divided; ever eaten, though never consumed, but sanctifying them that partake thereof.

On the Division of the Holy Lamb.

It is necessary for thee to know, O priest, that on breaking the Holy Lamb thou must place the part with the sign of the Cross downward on the holy diskos, the incised side upward, as before when it was cut. IC, therefore, is

вы́шнѣй странѣ̀ ст҃а́гѡ ді́скоса, ꙗ́же є҆́сть
на восто́цѣ: Хⷭ҇ же, ѿ до́лꙋ є҆́же є҆́сть на
за́падѣ: а̀ є҆́же НІ, ѿ сѣ́верныѧ страны̀,
КА же, съ полꙋ́денныѧ страны̀, ꙗ́коже здѣ̀
и҆з̾ѡбрази́сѧ.

Іи҃С ᲂу҆́бѡ ча́сть взе́мъ, и҆сполнѧ́й
ст҃ꙋ́ю ча́шꙋ. Хⷭ҇ же, ча́сть, раздроблѧ́й
сщ҃е́нникѡмъ и҆ дїа́конѡмъ. Ты̑ѧ же
двѣ̀ ча̑сти ст҃ы̑ѧ, є҆́же НІ, и҆ є҆́же КА,
прича́стникѡмъ да раздроблѧ́еши на
ча̑сти ма́лыѧ, є҆ли́кѡ бꙋ́детъ дово́льно по
разсмотрѣ́нїю твоемꙋ̀. А҆ ѿ ча̑сти престѣ́ѧ
бц҃ы, и҆лѝ девѧти́хъ чинѡ́въ ст҃ы́хъ, и҆лѝ
и҆ны́хъ є҆ли́кѡ во ст҃е́мъ ді́скосѣ сꙋ́ть,
ника́коже кого̀ да причасти́ши: то́чїю ѿ
двою̀ ча́стїю, ѡ҆ста́вшею ст҃а́гѡ а҆́гнца, да
причаща́еши.

Къ томꙋ́же тебѣ̀ вѣ́домо бꙋ́детъ и҆
ѡ҆ се́мъ, ꙗ́кѡ є҆гда̀ растворѧ́еши ст҃ы́мъ
ᲂу҆кро́пцемъ бж҃е́ственнꙋ́ю кро́вь влⷣчню,
тогда̀ да влива́еши съ разсмотрѣ́нїемъ,
є҆ли́кѡ бы́ти дово́льно всѣ̑мъ хотѧ́щымъ

placed at the upper side of the holy diskos, which is toward the east. And XC, at the bottom, which is toward the west; and that which is NI, upon the north side; and KA, on the south side, as is depicted here:

Taking the portion IC, therefore, place it into the holy chalice. And divide the portion XC among the priests and deacons. Divide the other two portions, namely NI and KA, among the communicants in small particles, as many as may be sufficient according to thine own estimation.

But of the portion of the most-holy Theotokos, or of the nine orders of saints, or any others which are upon the holy diskos, thou shalt in no wise commune anyone; only of the two portions which remain of the Holy Lamb shalt thou give in Communion.

Furthermore, be it known unto thee also concerning this: that when thou dost dilute with the holy warm water the Divine Blood of the Master, then thou shalt pour with

причаститисѧ. Та́кожде и ѿ вinȧ и воды̀, є҆гда̀ пробода́еши ст҃ый а҆́гнецъ, тогда̀ да влива́еши толикꙋ, є҆ли́кѡ бы́ти дово́льно всѣ́мъ: послѣ́дй же никакоже что̀ да влива́еши, но то́чїю ѿ растворе́нїѧ є҆ди́ною, є҆́же на Ст҃а̑ѧ ст҃ы̑мъ, и та́кѡ причаща́й всѣ́хъ ѿ си́хъ.

Дїа́конъ же, показꙋ́ѧ ѻ҆раре́мъ ст҃ый потир̀, глаго́летъ:

И҆спо́лни, влады́ко, ст҃ый потир̀.

Сꙗ́щенникъ же взе́мъ горѣ̀ лежа́цꙋю ча́стицꙋ, ꙗ҆́же, І҆и҃с, твори́тъ съ не́ю крⷭ҇тъ верхꙋ̀ ст҃а́гѡ потира, глаго́лѧ:

И҆сполне́нїе дх҃а ст҃а́гѡ.

И҆ та́кѡ влага́етъ во ст҃ый потир̀.

Дїа́конъ: А҆ми́нь.

И҆ прїе́млѧ теплотꙋ̀, глаго́летъ къ сꙗ́щенникꙋ:

discretion so that there be enough for all that desire to partake. So also the wine and water, when thou dost pierce the Holy Lamb, then thou art to pour at that time an amount sufficient for all; after this, thou shalt pour no more, but only that which is necessary for the dilution at: **Holy Things are for the holy**, and thus communicate all therefrom.

Then the deacon, pointing to the holy chalice with his orarion, says:

Fill the holy chalice, master.

The priest, taking the portion which lies at the top, that is, IC, makes a cross over the holy chalice therewith, saying:

The fullness of the Holy Spirit.

And thus places it in the holy chalice.

Deacon: **Amen.**

And taking the warm water, he says to the priest:

Блⷢ҇гослови̑, влады́ко, теплотꙋ̀.

Сщ҃е́нникъ же блⷢ҇гословлѧ́етъ, глаго́лѧ:

Блⷢ҇гослове́на теплота̀ ст҃ы́хъ твои́хъ, всегда̀, ны́нѣ и̑ при́снѡ, и̑ во вѣ́ки вѣкѡ́въ. А҆ми́нь.

И҆ дїа́конъ вливае́тъ, є҆ли́кѡ дово́льно, крⷭ҇тоѻбра́знѡ внꙋ́трь ст҃а́гѡ поти́ра, глаго́лѧ:

Теплота̀ вѣ́ры и҆спо́лнь дх҃а ст҃а́гѡ. А҆ми́нь.

И҆ ѿста́вивъ теплотꙋ̀, стои́тъ ма́лѡ пода́лѣ.

Сщ҃е́нникъ же глаго́летъ: Дїа́коне, приступѝ.

И҆ прише́дъ дїа́конъ твори́тъ покло́нъ блⷢ҇гоговѣ́йнѡ, просѧ̀ проще́нїѧ.

Сщ҃е́нникъ же держа̀ ст҃ы́й хлѣ́бъ, дае́тъ дїа́конꙋ: и̑ цѣлова́въ дїа́конъ подаю́щꙋю є҆мꙋ̀ рꙋ́кꙋ, прїе́млетъ ст҃ы́й хлѣ́бъ, глаго́лѧ:

Bless the warm water, master.

The priest blesses it, saying:

Blessed is the fervor of Thy saints, always, now and ever, and unto the ages of ages. Amen.

And the deacon pours the water in the shape of a cross into the holy chalice, as much as is necessary, saying:

The fervor of faith, full of the Holy Spirit. Amen.

And having set aside the warm water, he stands a little aside.

And the priest says: Deacon, draw nigh.

And approaching, the deacon makes a bow, reverently, asking forgiveness.

The priest, holding the Holy Bread, gives it to the deacon; and the deacon having kissed the hand of him that gives, receives the Holy Bread, saying:

Преподаждь мнѣ влⷣко, чⷭ҇тное и стⷪ҇е тѣло гдⷭ҇а и бга и спⷭ҇а нашегѡ іиса хрⷭ҇та.

Сщⷰ҇енникъ же глаголетъ: Имⷦ҇ъ, сщⷰ҇енно-дїаконꙋ преподаетсѧ чⷭ҇тное и стⷪ҇е и пречⷭ҇тое тѣло гдⷭ҇а и бга и спⷭ҇а нашегѡ іиса хрⷭ҇та, во ѿставленїе грѣхѡвъ є҆гѡ, и въ жизнь вѣчнꙋю.

И ѿходитъ дїаконъ созади стⷯ҇ыѧ трапезы, приклонивъ главꙋ, и молитсѧ ꙗкѡ и сщⷰ҇енникъ, глаголѧ: Вѣⷬ҇ую, гдⷭ҇и, и прочаѧ.

Подобнѣ вземъ и сщⷰ҇енникъ є҆динꙋ частицꙋ стⷶ҇гѡ хлѣба, глаголетъ:

Чⷭ҇тное и престⷪ҇е тѣло гдⷭ҇а и бга и спⷭ҇а нашегѡ іиса хрⷭ҇та преподаетсѧ мнѣ, имⷦ҇ъ, сщⷰ҇енникꙋ, во ѿставленїе грѣхѡвъ моихъ, и въ жизнь вѣчнꙋю.

И приклонивъ главꙋ молитсѧ, глаголѧ:

Вѣⷬ҇ую, гдⷭ҇и, и исповѣдую, ꙗкѡ ты̀ є҆си воистиннꙋ хрⷭ҇тосъ, снⷭ҇ъ бга живагѡ,

Impart unto me, master, the precious and holy Body of our Lord and God and Saviour Jesus Christ.

And the priest says: To the sacred Deacon N. is imparted the precious and holy and most pure Body of our Lord and God and Saviour Jesus Christ, unto the remission of his sins, and life everlasting.

And bowing his head, the deacon goes behind the Holy Table and prays as does the priest, saying: I believe, O Lord…, and the rest.

Likewise the priest, taking one portion of the Holy Bread, says:

The precious and most holy Body of our Lord and God and Saviour Jesus Christ is imparted unto me, the Priest N., unto the remission of my sins, and life everlasting.

And bowing his head, he prays, saying:

I believe, O Lord, and I confess that Thou art truly the Christ, the Son of the living God,

пришедый въ мі́ръ грѣ́шныѧ сп҃сти́, ѿ
ни́хже пе́рвый є҆́смь а҆́зъ. Є҆щѐ вѣ́рꙋю,
ꙗ҆́кѡ сїѐ са́мое є҆́сть пречⷭ҇тое тѣ́ло твоѐ,
и҆ сїѧ̀ сама́ѧ є҆́сть чтⷭ҇на́ѧ кро́вь твоѧ̀.
Молю́сѧ ᲂу҆́бо тебѣ̀: поми́лꙋй мѧ̀, и҆
прости́ ми прегрѣшє́нїѧ моѧ̑ во́льнаѧ
и҆ нево́льнаѧ, ꙗ҆̀же сло́вомъ, ꙗ҆̀же дѣ́ломъ,
ꙗ҆̀же вѣ́дѣнїемъ и҆ невѣ́дѣнїемъ: и҆ сподо́би
мѧ̀ неѡсꙋжде́ннѡ причасти́тисѧ пречⷭ҇тыхъ
твои́хъ та́инствъ, во ѡ҆ставле́нїе грѣхѡ́въ
и҆ въ жи́знь вѣ́чнꙋю. А҆ми́нь.

Та́же:

Ве́чери твоеѧ̀ та́йныѧ дне́сь, сн҃е бж҃їй,
прича́стника мѧ̀ прїими́: не бо̀ врагѡ́мъ
твои̑мъ та́йнꙋ повѣ́мъ, ни лобза́нїѧ
ти́ да́мъ ꙗ҆́кѡ і҆ꙋ́да, но ꙗ҆́кѡ разбо́йникъ
и҆сповѣ́даю тѧ̀: помѧни́ мѧ, гдⷭ҇и, во црⷭ҇твїи
твое́мъ.

Да не въ сꙋ́дъ и҆лѝ во ѡ҆сꙋжде́нїе бꙋ́детъ
мнѣ̀ причаще́нїе ст҃ы́хъ твои́хъ та́инъ, гдⷭ҇и,
но во и҆сцѣле́нїе дꙋшѝ и҆ тѣ́ла.

Who didst come into the world to save sinners of whom I am chief. Moreover, I believe that this is truly Thy most pure Body, and that this is truly Thine own precious Blood. Wherefore, I pray Thee: Have mercy on me and forgive me my transgressions, voluntary and involuntary, in word and deed, in knowledge and in ignorance. And vouchsafe me to partake without condemnation of Thy most pure Mysteries unto the remission of sins and life everlasting. Amen.

Then:

Of Thy Mystical Supper, O Son of God, receive me today as a communicant; for I will not speak of the Mystery to Thine enemies, nor will I give Thee a kiss as did Judas, but like the Thief do I confess Thee: Remember me, O Lord, in Thy kingdom.

Let not the communion of Thy holy Mysteries be unto me for judgment or condemnation, O Lord, but for healing of soul and body.

И та́кѡ причаща́ютсѧ въ рꙋка́хъ держи́магѡ со стра́хомъ и всѧ́цемъ ᲂу҆твержде́нїемъ.

Та́же сщ҃е́нникъ воста́въ, прїе́млетъ ᲂо҆бѣ́ма рꙋка́ма съ покро́вцемъ ст҃ы́й поти́ръ, и҆ причаща́етсѧ три́жды и҆з него̀, глаго́лѧ:

Чⷭ҇тны́ѧ и ст҃ы́ѧ кро́ве гдⷭ҇а и҆ бг҃а и҆ сп҃са на́шегѡ і҆и҃са хрⷭ҇та̀, причаща́юсѧ а҆́зъ ра́бъ бж҃їй, сщ҃е́нникъ и҆́мк҃ъ, во ѡ҆ставле́нїе грѣхѡ́въ мои́хъ и въ жи́знь вѣ́чнꙋю. А҆ми́нь.

И҆ та́кѡ свои̑ ᲂу҆стнѣ̀, и҆ кра́й сщ҃е́ннагѡ поти́ра въ рꙋкꙋ̀ держи́мымъ покро́вцемъ ѡ҆те́ръ, и҆ глаго́летъ:

Сѐ прикоснꙋ́сѧ ᲂу҆стна́мъ мои̑мъ, и҆ ѿи́метъ беззакѡ́нїѧ моѧ̀, и҆ грѣхѝ моѧ̀ ѡ҆чи́ститъ.

Та́же призыва́етъ дїа́кона, глаго́лѧ:

Дїа́коне, пристꙋпѝ.

И҆ дїа́конъ прихо́дитъ и҆ покланѧ́етсѧ є҆ди́ною, глаго́лѧ:

And thus they partake of that which they hold in their hands with fear and all heedfulness.

Then rising, the priest takes the holy chalice in both hands with the cloth, and partakes thrice from it, saying:

Of the precious and holy Blood of our Lord and God and Saviour Jesus Christ do I, the servant of God, the Priest N., partake unto the remission of my sins and life everlasting.

And thus, having wiped his lips and the holy chalice with the cloth that he holds in his hand, he says:

Behold, this hath touched my lips, and taketh away mine iniquities, and purgeth away my sins.

Then he calls the deacon, saying:

Deacon, draw nigh.

And the deacon approaches, and bows down once, saying:

Сѐ прихождꙋ̀ къ безсме́ртномꙋ цр҃ю̀ и҆ бг҃ꙋ на́шемꙋ.

Д҃: Преподажⷣь мѝ, влⷣы́ко, чⷭ҇тнꙋ́ю и҆ ст҃ꙋ́ю кро́вь гдⷭ҇а и҆ бг҃а и҆ сп҃са на́шегѡ і҆и҃са хрⷭ҇та̀.

И҆ глаго́летъ сщ҃е́нникъ:

Причаща́етсѧ ра́бъ бж҃їй, дїа́конъ и҆м҃къ, чⷭ҇тны́ѧ и҆ ст҃ы́ѧ кро́ве гдⷭ҇а и҆ бг҃а и҆ сп҃са на́шегѡ і҆и҃са хрⷭ҇та̀, во ѡ҆ставле́нїе грѣхѡ́въ свои́хъ и҆ въ жи́знь вѣ́чнꙋю.

Причасти́вшꙋсѧ же дїа́конꙋ, гл҃етъ сщ҃е́нникъ:

Сѐ прикоснꙋ́сѧ оу҆стна́мъ твои́мъ, и҆ ѿи́метъ беззакѡ́нїѧ твоѧ̀, и҆ грѣхѝ твоѧ̀ ѡ҆чи́ститъ.

Подоба́етъ вѣ́дати, ꙗ҆́кѡ а҆́ще сꙋ́ть хотѧ́щїи причаща́тисѧ ст҃ы́хъ та́инъ, раздробла́етъ сщ҃е́нникъ двѣ̀ ча́сти ст҃а́гѡ а҆́гнца ѡ҆ста́вшыѧ, є҆́же НІ, и҆ є҆́же КА, на ма́лыѧ ча́стицы, ꙗ҆́кѡ бы́ти всѣ́мъ

Behold, I approach unto the Immortal King and our God.

And: Impart unto me, master, the precious and holy Blood of our Lord and God and Saviour Jesus Christ.

And the priest says:

The servant of God, the Deacon N., partaketh of the precious and holy Blood of our Lord and God and Saviour Jesus Christ unto the remission of his sins and life everlasting.

The deacon having partaken, the priest says:

Behold, this hath touched thy lips, and taketh away thine iniquities, and purgeth away thy sins.

It should be known, that if there be those that desire to partake of the Holy Mysteries, the priest breaks the two portions of the Holy Lamb that remain, that is, NI and KA, into small pieces, so that there be sufficient for all

причⷶстникѡмъ довольно: и та́кѡ влага́етъ и҆́хъ во ст҃ꙋ́ю ча́шꙋ.

И҆ покрыва́етъ ст҃ы́й потирⷬ покро́вцемъ, подо́бнѣ и҆ на ст҃ы́й ді́скосъ возлага́етъ ѕвѣзди́цꙋ и҆ покро́вцы.

Та́же глаго́летъ мл҃твꙋ бл҃года́рственнꙋю сщ҃е́нникъ:

Бл҃года́римъ тѧ̀, влⷣко чл҃вѣколю́бче, бл҃годѣ́телю дꙋ́шъ на́шихъ: ꙗ҆́кѡ и҆ въ настоѧ́щїй де́нь сподо́билъ є҆сѝ на́съ нбⷭ҇ныхъ твои́хъ и҆ безсме́ртныхъ та́инствъ. И҆спра́ви на́шъ пꙋ́ть, оу҆тверди́ ны во стра́сѣ твое́мъ всѧ̑, соблюди́ на́шъ живо́тъ, оу҆тверди́ на́ша стѡпы̀, моли́твами и҆ моле́ньми сла́вныѧ бцⷣы и҆ приснодв҃ы мр҃і́и, и҆ всѣ́хъ ст҃ы́хъ твои́хъ.

И҆ та́кѡ ѿверза́ютъ две́ри ст҃а́гѡ ѻ҆лтарѧ̀. И҆ дїа́конъ, поклони́всѧ є҆ди́ною, прїе́млетъ потирⷬ со бл҃гогове́нїемъ, и҆ прихо́дитъ во две́ри, и҆ возносѧ̀ ст҃ы́й потирⷬ, показꙋ́етъ и҆́ лю́демъ, глаго́лѧ:

communicants, and then puts them into the
holy chalice.

And he covers the holy chalice with a veil,
and also places the star and veils upon the
holy diskos.

And the priest says this prayer of
thanksgiving:

We give thanks unto Thee, O Master,
lover of mankind, Benefactor of our
souls, that on this very day Thou hast vouchsafed unto us Thy heavenly and immortal
Mysteries. Direct our way, establish us all
in thy fear, preserve our life, make steadfast
our steps, through the intercessions and
supplications of the glorious Theotokos and
Ever-Virgin Mary and of all the saints.

And then they open the doors of the
holy altar. And the deacon, bowing once,
receives the holy chalice with reverence, and
approaches the doors, and elevating the holy
chalice, shows it to the people, saying:

Со стра́хомъ бж҃інмъ и вѣ́рою пристꙋ́пите.

Ли́къ: Бл҃гослове́нъ гряды́й во и́мѧ гдⷭне, бг҃ъ гдⷭь, и ꙗ҆ви́сѧ на́мъ.

Та́же пристꙋ́паютъ хотѧ́щїи причаща́тисѧ. И҆ и́дꙋтъ є҆ди́нъ по є҆ди́номꙋ, и покланѧ́ютсѧ со всѧ́цѣмъ оу҆миле́нїемъ и҆ стра́хомъ, согбе́ннѣ рꙋ́цѣ къ пе́рсемъ и҆мꙋ́ще: та́же прїе́млетъ кі́ждо бж҃е́ственныя та́йны.

Сщ҃е́нникъ же, причаща́ѧ є҆гѡ̀, глаго́летъ:

Причаща́етсѧ ра́бъ бж҃їй и́мⷬкъ, чтⷭна́гѡ и҆ ст҃а́гѡ тѣ́ла и҆ кро́ве гдⷭа и҆ бг҃а и҆ сп҃са на́шегѡ і҆и҃са хрⷭта̀, во ѡ҆ставле́нїе грѣхѡ́въ и҆ въ жи́знь вѣ́чнꙋю.

И҆ дїа́конъ ѡ҆тира́етъ є҆мꙋ̀ оу҆стнѣ̀ пла́томъ, и҆ цѣлꙋ́етъ причасти́выйсѧ ст҃ꙋ́ю ча́шꙋ, и҆ поклони́всѧ ѿхо́дитъ.

И҆ та́кѡ причаща́ютсѧ всѝ.

With fear of God and with faith draw nigh.
Choir: Blessed is He that cometh in the
name of the Lord. God is the Lord, and hath
appeared unto us.

Then those that desire to partake draw nigh.
And they come one by one, and bow down
with all compunction and fear, having their
arms folded on their breast. Then each one
receives the Divine Mysteries.

The priest, as he communicates every one,
says:

The servant [or handmaiden] of God N.,
partaketh of the precious and holy Body
and Blood of our Lord and God and Saviour
Jesus Christ, unto the remission of sins and
life everlasting.

And the deacon wipes the communicant's
lips with the cloth, and the communicant
kisses the holy chalice, and bowing,
withdraws.

And in this manner do all partake.

По причаще́нїи же, вхо́дитъ їере́й
во ст҃ы́й ѻлта́рь, и̑ поставлѧ́етъ ст҃а̑ѧ
на ст҃е́мъ пⷬ҇то́лѣ. Тогда̀ прїе́мъ
дїа́конъ ст҃ы́й ді́скосъ верхꙋ̀ ст҃а́гѡ
потира, и̑ глаго́лѧ воскр҃ны̑ѧ
пѣ̑сни сїѧ̑:

Воскрⷭ҇нїе хрⷭ҇то́во ви́дѣвше, поклони́мсѧ
ст҃о́мꙋ гдⷭ҇ꙋ і̑и҃ꙋ, є̑ди́номꙋ безгрѣ́шномꙋ.
крⷭ҇тꙋ̀ твоемꙋ̀ покланѧ́емсѧ, хрⷭ҇тѐ, и̑ ст҃о́е
воскрⷭ҇нїе твоѐ пое́мъ и̑ сла́вимъ: ты́ бо є̑сѝ
бг҃ъ на́шъ, ра́звѣ тебѐ и̑но́гѡ не зна́емъ,
и̑мѧ твоѐ и̑менꙋ́емъ. Прїиди́те всѝ вѣ́рнїи,
поклони́мсѧ ст҃о́мꙋ хрⷭ҇то́вꙋ воскрⷭ҇нїю: се́ бо
прїи́де крⷭ҇то́мъ ра́дость всемꙋ̀ мі́рꙋ. Всегда̀
бл҃гословѧ́ще гдⷭ҇а, пое́мъ воскрⷭ҇нїе є̑гѡ̀:
распѧ́тїе бо претерпѣ́въ, сме́ртїю сме́рть
разрꙋ́ши.

Свѣти́сѧ, свѣти́сѧ, но́вый і̑ерⷭ҇ли́ме,
сла́ва бо гдⷭ҇нѧ на тебѣ̀ возсїѧ̀. Ликꙋ́й
ны́нѣ, и̑ весел и́сѧ сїѡ́не: ты́ же, чⷭ҇таѧ,
красꙋ́йсѧ, бц҃е, ѡ̑ воста́нїи ржⷭ҇тва̀ твоегѡ̀.

After communion, the priest enters the holy altar and places the Holy Things upon the Holy Table. The deacon then holds the holy diskos over the holy chalice [while placing the particles into the chalice], and says these hymns:

Having beheld the Resurrection of Christ, let us worship the holy Lord Jesus, the Only Sinless One. We worship Thy Cross, O Christ, and Thy holy Resurrection we hymn and glorify, for Thou art our God, and we know none other beside Thee; we call upon Thy name. O come, all ye faithful, let us worship Christ's holy Resurrection, for behold, through the Cross, joy hath come to all the world. Ever blessing the Lord, we hymn His Resurrection, for having endured crucifixion, He hath destroyed death by death.

Shine, shine, O new Jerusalem, for the glory of the Lord has shone upon thee; dance now, and be glad, O Sion; and do thou

Ѽ па́сха ве́лїѧ и҆ сщ҃е́ннѣйшаѧ, хрⷭ҇тѐ! Ѽ мꙋ́дросте, и҆ сло́ве бж҃їй, и҆ си́ло! подава́й на́мъ и҆́стѣе тебѐ причаща́тисѧ, въ невече́рнѣмъ дни̑ црⷭ҇тв́їѧ твоегѡ̀.

Ѡ҆тира́етъ ст҃о́ю гꙋ́бою ѕѣлѡ̀ до́брѣ, со внима́нїемъ и҆ бл҃гоговѣ́нїемъ, глаго́лѧ словеса̀ сїѧ̑:

Ѡ҆мы́й, гдⷭ҇и, грѣхѝ помина́вшихсѧ здѣ̀ кро́вїю твое́ю чтⷭ҇но́ю, мл҃твами ст҃ы́хъ твои́хъ.

Сщ҃е́нникъ же бл҃гословлѧ́етъ лю́ди, возглаша́ѧ:

Сп҃сѝ, бж҃е, лю́ди твоѧ̑, и҆ бл҃гословѝ достоѧ́нїе твоѐ.

И҆ ѡ҆браща́етсѧ сщ҃е́нникъ ко ст҃ѣ́й трапе́зѣ, и҆ кади́тъ сщ҃е́нникъ три́жды, глаго́лѧ въ себѣ̀:

exult, O pure Theotokos, in the arising of Him Whom thou didst bear.

O great and most sacred Pascha, O Christ! O Wisdom, and Word of God, and Power! Grant us more perfectly to partake of Thee, in the unwaning day of Thy kingdom.

The deacon wipes [the diskos] with the holy sponge exceedingly well, with attentiveness and reverence, saying these words:

Wash away by Thy precious Blood, O Lord, the sins of those here commemorated, through the prayers of Thy saints.

And the priest blesses the people, exclaiming:

Save, O God, Thy people, and bless Thine inheritance.

And the priest turns back to the Holy Table, and censes it thrice, saying within himself:

Вознеси́сѧ на нб҃са̀, бж҃е, и҆ по все́й землѝ сла́ва твоѧ̀.

Ли́къ же пое́тъ: Ви́дехомъ свѣ́тъ и҆́стинный, прїѧ́хомъ дх҃а нб҃наго, ѡ҆брѣ́тохомъ вѣ́рꙋ и҆́стиннꙋю, неразлꙋ́чнѣй трⷪ҇цѣ покланѧ́емсѧ: та́ бо на́съ спасла̀ є҆́сть.

Та́же взе́мъ сщ҃е́нникъ ст҃ы́й ді́скосъ, возлага́етъ на главꙋ̀ дїа́кона, и҆ дїа́конъ прїе́мъ и҆̀ со бл҃гоговѣ́нїемъ, зрѧ̀ внѣ̀ къ две́ремъ, ничто́же глаго́лѧ, ѿхо́дитъ въ предложе́нїе, и҆ поставлѧ́етъ и҆̀.

Сщ҃е́нникъ же поклони́всѧ, и҆ прїе́мъ ст҃ы́й поти́ръ, и҆ ѡ҆бра́щьсѧ къ две́ремъ, зрѧ̀ на лю́ди, глаго́летъ та́йнѡ:

Бл҃гослове́нъ бг҃ъ на́шъ:

И҆ возгла́снѡ: Всегда̀, ны́нѣ и҆ при́снѡ, и҆ во вѣ́ки вѣкѡ́въ.

И҆ ѿхо́дитъ ко ст҃о́мꙋ предложе́нїю и҆ поставлѧ́етъ та́мѡ ст҃а҄ѧ.

Be Thou exalted above the heavens, O God,
and Thy glory above all the earth.

Choir: We have seen the true Light, we have
received the Heavenly Spirit, we have found
the True Faith. We worship the indivisible
Trinity, for He hath saved us.

Then the priest takes the holy diskos,
places it on the deacon's head, and the
deacon receives it with reverence; looking
out through the doors, saying nothing, he
goes to the table of oblation and places it
thereon.

The priest bows, and takes the holy chalice,
and turning to the doors, looking toward
the people, he says secretly:

Blessed is our God,
And aloud: Always, now and ever, and unto
the ages of ages.

And he goes to the holy table of oblation
and places the Holy Things on it.

Ли́къ: А҆ми́нь. Да и҆спо́лнѧтсѧ ᲂу҆ста̀ на́ша хвале́нїѧ твоегѡ̀, гд҃и, ꙗ҆́кѡ да пое́мъ сла́вꙋ твою̀, ꙗ҆́кѡ сподо́билъ є҆сѝ на́съ причасти́тисѧ ст҃ы́мъ твои́мъ, бж҃е́ственнымъ, безсме́ртнымъ и҆ животворѧ́щымъ та́йнамъ: соблюдѝ на́съ во твое́й ст҃ы́ни, ве́сь де́нь поꙋча́тисѧ пра́вдѣ твое́й. А҆ллилꙋ́їа, а҆ллилꙋ́їа, а҆ллилꙋ́їа.

И҆ и҆зше́дъ дїа́конъ се́верною две́рїю, и҆ ста́въ на ᲂу҆бы́чномъ мѣ́стѣ, глаго́летъ:

Про́сти прїи́мше бж҃е́ственныхъ, ст҃ы́хъ, пречⷭ҇тыхъ, безсме́ртныхъ, нбⷭ҇ныхъ и҆ животворѧ́щихъ, стра́шныхъ хрⷭ҇то́выхъ та́йнъ, досто́йнѡ бл҃годари́мъ гдⷭ҇а.

Ли́къ: Гдⷭ҇и, поми́лꙋй.

Дїа́конъ: Застꙋпѝ, спасѝ, поми́лꙋй и҆ сохранѝ на́съ, бж҃е, твое́ю бл҃года́тїю.

Ли́къ: Гдⷭ҇и, поми́лꙋй.

Дїа́конъ: Де́нь ве́сь соверше́нъ, ст҃ъ, ми́ренъ и҆ безгрѣ́шенъ и҆спроси́вше, са́ми себѐ и҆ дрꙋ́гъ дрꙋ́га, и҆ ве́сь живо́тъ на́шъ хрⷭ҇тꙋ̀ бг҃ꙋ предади́мъ.

Ли́къ: Тебѣ̀, гдⷭ҇и.

Choir: Amen. Let our mouth be filled with Thy praise, O Lord, that we may hymn Thy glory, for Thou hast vouchsafed us to partake of Thy holy, divine, immortal and life-giving Mysteries. Keep us in Thy holiness, that we may meditate on Thy righteousness all the day long. Alleluia, alleluia, alleluia.

And the deacon comes out by the north door, and standing in the usual place, says:

Aright! Having partaken of the divine, holy, most pure, immortal, heavenly, and life-giving, fearful Mysteries of Christ, let us worthily give thanks unto the Lord.

Choir: Lord, have mercy.

Deacon: Help us, save us, have mercy on us, and keep us, O God, by Thy grace.

Choir: Lord, have mercy.

Deacon: Having asked that the whole day may be perfect, holy, peaceful and sinless, let us commit ourselves and one another and all our life unto Christ, our God.

Choir: To Thee, O Lord.

Їере́й же, согну́въ антїми́нсъ и пра́мѡ
держа̀ є҆ѵⷢлїе, твори́тъ над ни́мъ крⷭтъ, и̑
возглаша́етъ:

Ꙗ҆́кѡ ты̀ є҆сѝ ѡ҆сщ҃е́нїе на́ше, и̑ тебѣ̀ сла́ву
возсыла́емъ, ѻ҆ц҃у̀, и̑ сн҃у, и̑ ст҃о́му дх҃у,
ны́нѣ и̑ при́снѡ, и̑ во вѣ́ки вѣкѡ́въ.

   Ли́къ: А҆ми́нь.

Їере́й: Съ ми́ромъ и҆зы́демъ.

   Ли́къ: Ѡ҆ и҆́мени гдⷭни.

Дїа́конъ: Гдⷭу помо́лимсѧ.

   Ли́къ: Гдⷭи, помилу́й.

Мл҃тва заамвѡ́ннаѧ возгла́снѡ глаго́летсѧ
ѿ і҆ере́а:

Б҃лгословлѧ́ай бл҃гословѧ́щыѧ тѧ̀, гдⷭи,
и̑ ѡ҆сщ҃а́й на тѧ̀ ѹ҆пова́ющыѧ, сп҃сѝ
лю́ди твоѧ̑, и̑ бл҃гословѝ достоѧ́нїе твоѐ,
и҆сполне́нїе цр҃кве твоеѧ̀ сохранѝ, ѡ҆сти̑
любѧ́щыѧ бл҃голѣ́пїе до́му твоегѡ̀: ты̀

The priest, having folded the antimension, and holding the Gospel upright, before laying it upon the antimension, makes the sign of the cross with it over the antimension and exclaims:

For Thou art our sanctification, and unto Thee do we send up glory, to the Father, and to the Son, and to the Holy Spirit, now and ever, and unto the ages of ages.

Choir: Amen.

Priest: Let us depart in peace.

Choir: In the name of the Lord.

Deacon: Let us pray to the Lord.

Choir: Lord, have mercy.

The priest says the Prayer behind the ambo aloud:

O Lord, Who dost bless them that bless Thee and sanctify them that put their trust in Thee: save Thy people and bless Thine inheritance. Preserve the fullness of Thy Church, sanctify them that love the

тѣхъ воспрослави бжⷭ҇твенною твоею силою, и не ѡстави насъ оу҆повающихъ на тѧ. Миръ мірови твоемꙋ да́рꙋй, цр҃квамъ твои̑мъ, сщ҃е́нникѡмъ, и̑ всѣ́мъ лю́демъ твои̑мъ. Ꙗ҆кѡ всѧ́кое даѧ́нїе бл҃го, и̑ всѧ́къ да́ръ совершенъ свы́ше е҆́сть, сходѧ́й ѿ тебе ѻ҆ц҃а̀ свѣ́тѡвъ: и̑ тебѣ̀ сла́вꙋ, и̑ бл҃годаре́нїе, и̑ поклоне́нїе возсыла́емъ, ѻ҆ц҃ꙋ, и̑ сн҃ꙋ, и̑ ст҃о́мꙋ дх҃ꙋ, ны́нѣ и̑ при́снѡ, и̑ во вѣ́ки вѣкѡ́въ.

Ли́къ: А҆ми́нь.

Та́же: Бꙋ́ди и̑мѧ гдⷭ҇не: три́жды и̑ ѱало́мъ л҃г, Бл҃гословлю̀ гдⷭ҇а:

Моли́твѣ же глаго́лемѣй, дїа́конъ сто́итъ на десно́й странѣ̀ пред ѻ҆бразомъ влⷣки хрⷭ҇та̀, держа̀ и̑ ѻ҆ра́рь свой, главꙋ̀ приклонь, до соверше́нїѧ мл҃твы: се́й же скончавшейсѧ, сщ҃е́нникъ оу҆́бѡ входитъ

beauty of Thy house. Do Thou glorify them by Thy divine power, and forsake us not that hope in Thee. Give peace to Thy world, to Thy churches, to the priests, and to all Thy people. For every good gift and every perfect gift is from above and cometh down from Thee, the Father of lights, and unto Thee do we send up glory and thanksgiving and worship: to the Father, and to the Son, and to the Holy Spirit, now and ever, and unto the ages of ages.

Choir: Amen.

Also the choir: Blessed be the Name of the Lord ... (thrice), and Psalm 33: I will bless the Lord ...

While the Prayer behind the ambo is being said, the deacon stands on the right side before the icon of Christ the Master, holding his orarion, head bowed, until the completion of the Prayer. This being concluded, the priest then enters through

ст҃ыми две́рьми, и҆ ѿше́дъ въ предложе́нїе, глаго́летъ настоѧ́щꙋю мл҃твꙋ:

Мл҃тва, глаго́лемаѧ внегда̀ потреби́ти ст҃а҃ѧ:

И҆сполне́нїе зако́на и҆ прⷪ҇ро́кѡвъ са́мъ сы́й, хрⷭ҇тѐ бж҃е на́шъ, и҆спо́лнивый всѐ ѻ҆́ческое смотре́нїе, и҆спо́лни ра́дости и҆ весе́лїѧ сердца̀ на́шѧ, всегда̀, ны́нѣ и҆ прⷭ҇нѡ, и҆ во вѣ́ки вѣкѡ́въ.

Дїа́конъ же вше́дъ сѣ́верною страно́ю, потребля́етъ ст҃а҃ѧ со стра́хомъ, и҆ со всѧ́кимъ ѹ҆твержде́нїемъ.

Сщ҃е́нникъ глаго́летъ:

Блгⷭ҇ове́нїе гдⷭ҇не на ва́съ, тогѡ̀ блгⷣтїю и҆ чл҃вѣколю́бїемъ, всегда̀, ны́нѣ и҆ прⷭ҇нѡ, и҆ во вѣ́ки вѣкѡ́въ.

Ли́къ: А҆ми́нь.

the holy doors, and having gone to the table
of oblation, he says the following prayer:

The Prayer said when the Holy Things are
to be consumed:

Thou Who thyself art the fulfillment of the
law and the prophets, O Christ our God,
Who didst fulfill all the Father's dispensation, fill our hearts with joy and gladness,
always, now and ever, and unto the ages of
ages.

The deacon, having entered by the north
side, consumes the Holy Things with fear
and with all heedfulness.

The priest says:

The blessing of the Lord be upon you,
through His grace and love for mankind,
always, now and ever, and unto the ages of
ages.

Choir: Amen.

Сщ҃е́нникъ: Сла́ва тебѣ̀, хрⷵтѐ бж҃е, ѹ҆пова́нїе на́ше, сла́ва тебѣ̀.

Ли́къ: Сла́ва, и҆ ны́нѣ: Гдⷵи, поми́лꙋй, три́жды. Бл҃гословѝ.

Сщ҃е́нникъ: Хрⷵто́съ и҆́стинный бг҃ъ на́шъ, мл҃твами пречⷵтыѧ своеѧ̀ мт҃ре [и҆ прⷪ҇чаѧ], и҆́же во ст҃ы́хъ ѻ҆ц҃а̀ на́шегѡ і҆ѡа́нна, а҆рхїе҆пкⷵпа кѡнстанті́на гра́да, златоꙋ́стагѡ: и҆ ст҃а́гѡ и҆́мⷦ҇ъ, [е҆гѡ́же е҆́сть хра́мъ и҆ е҆гѡ́же е҆́сть де́нь:], и҆ всѣ́хъ ст҃ы́хъ, поми́лꙋетъ и҆ сп҃се́тъ на́съ, ꙗ҆́кѡ бл҃гъ и҆ чл҃вѣколю́бецъ.

Ли́къ: А҆ми́нь.

Ли́къ же многолѣ́тствꙋетъ.

Сщ҃е́нникъ же и҆зше́дъ, дае́тъ лю́демъ а҆нті́дѡръ.

Та́же сщ҃е́нникъ, вше́дъ во ст҃ы́й ѻ҆лта́рь, глаго́летъ бл҃года́рныѧ мл҃твы [страни́ца ѕ҃і].

Та́же: Ны́нѣ ѿпꙋща́еши: Трист҃о́е. И҆ по Ѻ҆́че на́шъ:

Priest: Glory to Thee, O Christ God, our hope, glory to Thee.

Choir: Glory, both now ... Lord, have mercy, (thrice). Father, bless.

Priest: May Christ our true God, through the intercessions of His most pure Mother [and the rest]; of our father among the saints John Chrysostom, archbishop of Constantinople; of Saint(s) N.: [whose temple it is and whose day it is] and of all the Saints, have mercy on us and save us, for He is good and the Lover of mankind.

Choir: Amen.

And the choir sings the Polychronion.

And the priest, having gone out, gives antidoron to the people.

Then, the priest, having entered the holy altar says the thanksgiving prayers [page 247].

Then, Now lettest Thou... The Trisagion. And after Our Father:

Ѿпꙋстительный тропа́рь, гла́съ и҃:

Оу҆́стъ твои́хъ ꙗ҆́коже свѣ́тлость о҆гнѧ̀
возсїѧ́вши блгода́ть, вселе́ннꙋю просвѣтѝ:
не сребролю́бїѧ мі́рови сокрѡ́вища сниска̀,
высотꙋ̀ на́мъ смиренномꙋ́дрїѧ показа̀: но
твои́ми словесы̀ наказꙋ́ѧ, о҆́тче і҆ѡа́нне
златоꙋ́сте, молѝ сло́ва хрⷭ҇та̀ бга, сп҃сти́сѧ
дꙋша́мъ на́шымъ.

Сла́ва: Конда́къ, гла́съ ѕ҃.

Подо́бенъ: Е҆́же ѿ на́съ:

Ѿ нб҃съ прїѧ́лъ є҆сѝ бжⷭ҇твеннꙋю блгода́ть,
и҆ твои́ма оу҆стна́ма всѧ̑ оу҆чи́ши поклана́-
тисѧ въ трⷪ҇цѣ є҆ди́номꙋ бгꙋ, і҆ѡа́нне
златоꙋ́сте, всеблаже́нне прпⷣбне, досто́йнѡ
хва́лимъ тѧ̀: є҆сѝ бо наста́вникъ, ꙗ҆́кѡ
бжⷭ҇твеннаѧ ꙗ҆влѧ́ѧ.

И҆ ны́нѣ, бг҃оро́диченъ:

Предста́тельство хрⷭ҇тїа́нъ непосты́дное,
хода́тайство ко творцꙋ̀ непрело́жное,
не пре́зри грѣ́шныхъ моле́нїй гла́сы: но
предварѝ, ꙗ҆́кѡ блга́ѧ, на по́мощь на́съ,

Troparion, 8th tone:

Grace like a flame shining forth from Thy mouth hath illumined the universe, and disclosed to the world treasures of uncovetousness, and shown us the heights of humility; but while instructing us by Thy words, O Father John Chrysostom, intercede with the word, Christ our God, to save our souls.

Glory... Kontakion, 6th tone:

Prosomion: When Thou didst fulfill:

From the heavens hast thou received divine grace, and by thy lips thou dost teach all to worship the One God in Trinity, O John Chrysostom, all-blessed righteous one. Rightly do we acclaim thee, for thou art a teacher revealing things divine.

Both now... Theotokion:

O protection of Christians that cannot be put to shame, O mediation unto the Creator unfailing: disdain not the suppliant voices of sinners; but be thou quick, O good one,

вѣ́рнѡ зовꙋ́щихъ тѧ̀: оу҆скорѝ на мл҃твꙋ̀,
и҆ потщи́сѧ на оу҆моле́нїе, предста́тельст_
вꙋ́ющи при́снѡ, бцⷣе, чтꙋ́щихъ тѧ̀.

И҆лѝ а҆́ще хо́щеши,
рцы̀ и҆ дню̀ тропа́рь.

Гдⷭи, поми́лꙋй, в҃і.
Честнѣ́йшꙋю:

Сла́ва, и҆ ны́нѣ:
и҆ твори́тъ ѿпꙋ́стъ.

Потреби́вшꙋ же дїа́конꙋ ст҃а̑ѧ со
всѧ́цѣмъ ѿпасе́нїемъ, ꙗ҆́кѡ ничемꙋ̀ ѿ
ст҃ы́хъ дробнѣ́йшихъ па́сти крꙋпи́цъ, и҆лѝ
ѡ҆ста́тисѧ, налїа́въ во ст҃ꙋ́ю ча́шꙋ ѿ вїна̀ и҆
воды̀, и҆ потреби́въ, и҆ сопра́тавъ гꙋ́бою всю̀
мокротꙋ̀.

Та́же слага́етъ ст҃ы̑ѧ сосꙋ́ды вкꙋ́пѣ, и҆
ѡ҆бвѧза́въ а҆̀хъ, полага́етъ на ѻ҆бы́чномъ
мѣ́стѣ, глаго́ла: Ны́нѣ ѿпꙋща́еши: и҆

to help us who in faith cry unto thee; hasten to intercession and speed thou to make supplication, thou who dost ever protect, O Theotokos, them that honor thee.

Or, if thou wilt,
say the troparion of the day.

Lord, have mercy (twelve times).
More honorable…

Glory… Both now…
And he gives the dismissal.

The deacon, having consumed the Holy Things with all diligence, so that no smallest particle fall or remain, pours into the holy chalice some wine and water, and consumes it, and wipes away all moisture with the sponge.

Then he puts the holy vessels together, and wrapping them, sets them in their usual place, saying: Now lettest Thou, and the

прⷰ҇чⷶ҇л, ꙗ́коже и҆ сщ҃е́нникъ. И҆ ѿмыва́етъ рꙋки на ѻ҆бы́чномъ мѣ́стѣ, и҆ поклони́всѧ вкꙋ́пѣ со сщ҃е́нникомъ, творѧ́тъ ѿпꙋ́стъ, и҆ бл҃годарѧ́ще бг҃а ѡ҆ всѣ́хъ, и҆схо́дѧтъ.

Коне́цъ бж҃е́ственныѧ литꙋргі́и ст҃а́гѡ і҆ѡа́нна златоꙋ́стагѡ.

rest, as did the priest, and washes his hands
in the usual place, and bowing together
with the priest, they make the dismissal,
and giving thanks unto God for all things,
they depart.

The End of the Divine Liturgy
of St. John Chrysostom

Мл҃твы бл҃года́рственныѧ по ст҃ѣ́мъ причаще́нїи

Є҆гда́ же полꙋчи́ши до́брагѡ причаще́нїѧ животворѧ́щихъ та́инственныхъ дарова́нїй, воспо́й а҆́бїе, бл҃годарѝ вельмѝ, и҆ сїѧ̀ те́плѣ ѿ дꙋшѝ бг҃ꙋ глаго́ли:

Сла́ва тебѣ̀, бж҃е. Сла́ва тебѣ̀, бж҃е. Сла́ва тебѣ̀, бж҃е.

Та́же бл҃года́рственнꙋю сїю̀ мл҃твꙋ:

Бл҃годарю́ тѧ, гдⷭ҇и бж҃е мо́й, ꙗ҆́кѡ не ѿри́нꙋлъ мѧ̀ є҆сѝ грѣ́шнаго, но ѻ҆́бщника мѧ̀ бы́ти ст҃ы́нь твои́хъ сподо́билъ є҆сѝ. Бл҃годарю́ тѧ, ꙗ҆́кѡ менѐ недосто́йнаго причасти́тисѧ пречⷭ҇ты́хъ твои́хъ и҆ нбⷭ҇ныхъ дарѡ́въ сподо́билъ є҆сѝ. Но, влⷣко чл҃вѣколю́бче, на́съ ра́ди ѹ҆ме́рый же и҆ воскрⷭ҇ый, и҆ дарова́вый на́мъ стра́шнаѧ сїѧ̑ и҆ животворѧ́щаѧ та́инства во бл҃годѣѧ́нїе и҆ ѡ҆сщ҃е́нїе дꙋ́шъ и҆ тѣле́съ на́шихъ, да́ждь бы́ти си̑мъ и҆ мнѣ̀

Prayers of Thanksgiving
After Communion

When you will have received the good
Communion of the life-giving Mystical
Gifts, give praise at once, give thanks
greatly, and from the soul say fervently
unto God these things:

Glory to Thee, O God. Glory to Thee, O
God. Glory to Thee, O God.

Then this Prayer of Thanksgiving:

I thank Thee, O Lord my God, that Thou
hast not rejected me, a sinner, but hast
vouchsafed me to be a communicant of Thy
Holy Things. I thank Thee that Thou hast
vouchsafed me, the unworthy, to partake
of Thy most pure and heavenly Gifts. But,
O Master, Lover of mankind, Who for our
sake didst die and didst rise again, and didst
bestow upon us these dread and life-giving
Mysteries for the well-being and sanctifica-

во исцѣле́нїе дꙋши́ же и тѣ́ла, во ѿгна́нїе
вся́кагѡ сопроти́внагѡ, въ просвѣще́нїе
о҆́чїю се́рдца моегѡ̀, въ ми́ръ дꙋше́вныхъ
мои́хъ си́лъ, въ вѣ́рꙋ непосты́днꙋ, въ любо́вь
нелицемѣ́рнꙋ, во исполне́нїе премꙋ́дрости,
въ соблюде́нїе за́повѣдей твои́хъ, въ
приложе́нїе бж҃е́ственныя твоея̀ бл҃года́ти,
и҆ твоегѡ̀ цр҃твїа присвое́нїе: да во ст҃ы́ни
твое́й тѣ́ми сохраня́емь, твою̀ бл҃года́ть
помина́ю всегда̀, и҆ не ктомꙋ̀ себѣ̀ живꙋ̀,
но тебѣ̀ на́шемꙋ влⷣцѣ и҆ бл҃годѣ́телю, и҆
та́кѡ сегѡ̀ житїа̀ и҆зше́дъ ѿ наде́жди
живота̀ вѣ́чнагѡ, въ присносꙋ́щный
дости́гнꙋ поко́й, и҆дѣ́же пра́зднꙋющихъ
гла́съ непреста́нный, и҆ безконе́чная
сла́дость, зря́щихъ твоегѡ̀ лица̀ добротꙋ̀
неизрече́ннꙋю: ты́ бо є҆сѝ и҆́стинное жела́нїе
и҆ неизрече́нное весе́лїе лю́бящихъ тѧ̀, хрⷭ҇тѐ
бж҃е на́шъ, и҆ тѧ̀ пое́тъ вся̀ тва́рь во
вѣ́ки. А҆ми́нь.

tion of our souls and bodies, grant that these may be even unto me for the healing of both soul and body, for the averting of everything hostile, for the enlightenment of the eyes of my heart, for the peace of the powers of my soul, for faith unashamed, for love unfeigned, for the fullness of wisdom, for the keeping of Thy commandments, for an increase of Thy divine grace, and for the attainment of Thy Kingdom; that being preserved by Them in Thy holiness, I may always remember Thy grace, and no longer live for myself, but for Thee our Master and Benefactor; and thus when I shall have departed this life in hope of life eternal, I may attain unto everlasting rest, where the sound of them that keep festival is unceasing, and the delight is endless of them that behold the ineffable beauty of Thy countenance. For Thou art the true desire and the unutterable gladness of them that love Thee, O Christ our God, and all creation doth hymn Thee unto the ages. Amen.

Вели́кагѡ Васі́лїа, втора́ѧ:

Влⷣко хрⷵтѐ бж҃е, цр҃ю вѣкѡ́въ и҆ содѣ́телю всѣ́хъ, бл҃годарю́ тѧ ѡ҆ всѣ́хъ, ꙗ҆́же мѝ є҆сѝ по́далъ бл҃ги́хъ, и҆ ѡ҆ причащенїи преⷱⷵтыхъ и҆ животворѧ́щихъ твои́хъ та́инствъ. Молю̀ ѹ҆̀бѡ тѧ̀, бл҃же и҆ чл҃вѣколю́бче: сохранѝ мѧ под кро́вомъ твои́мъ и҆ въ сѣ́ни крилꙋ̀ твоє́ю, и҆ дарꙋ́й мѝ чи́стою со́вѣстїю, да́же до послѣ́днагѡ моегѡ̀ и҆здыха́нїа, досто́йнѡ причаща́тисѧ ст҃ы́нь твои́хъ во ѡ҆ставле́нїе грѣхѡ́въ и҆ въ жи́знь вѣчнꙋ́ю. Ты́ бо є҆сѝ хлѣ́бъ живо́тный, и҆сто́чникъ ст҃ы́ни, пода́тель бл҃ги́хъ: и҆ тебѣ̀ сла́вꙋ возсыла́емъ, со ѻ҆ц҃е́мъ, и҆ ст҃ымъ дх҃омъ, нн҃ѣ и҆ при́снѡ и҆ во вѣ́ки вѣкѡ́въ. А҆ми́нь.

Метафра́ста по стїхѡ́мъ, тре́тїѧ.

Да́вый пи́щꙋ мнѣ̀ пло́ть твою̀ во́лею, ѻ҆́гнь сы́й, и҆ ѡ҆палѧ́ѧй недосто́йныѧ, да не ѡ҆пали́ши менѐ, содѣ́телю мо́й. Па́че же пройдѝ во ѹ҆́ды моѧ̑, во всѧ̑ соста́вы,

Of Basil the Great, 2:

O Master Christ God, King of the ages, and Creator of all things, I thank Thee for all the good things which Thou hast bestowed upon me, and for the communion of Thy most pure and life-giving Mysteries. I pray Thee, therefore, O Good One and Lover of mankind: Keep me under Thy protection and in the shadow of Thy wings and grant me, even until my last breath, to partake worthily, with a pure conscience, of Thy holy Things, unto the remission of sins and life eternal. For Thou art the Bread of Life, the Source of holiness, the Giver of good things; and unto Thee do we send up glory, together with the Father and the Holy Spirit, now and ever, and to the ages of ages. Amen.

Verses of Metaphrastes, 3:

O Thou Who givest me willingly Thy Flesh as food, Thou Who art fire that doth consume the unworthy, burn me not, O my Creator;

во оу҆тро́бꙋ, въ се́рдце. Попали́ те́рнïе
всѣ́хъ мои́хъ прегрѣше́нïй. Дꙋ́шꙋ ѡ҆чи́сти,
ѡ҆ст҃и́ помышлéнïѧ. Соста́вы оу҆тверди́
съ кость́ми вкꙋ́пѣ. Чꙋ́вствъ просвѣти́
просто́ю пѧтери́цꙋ. Всего́ мѧ спригвозди́
страхꙋ̀ твоемꙋ̀. При́снѡ покры́й, соблюди́
же и҆ сохрани́ мѧ ѿ вса́кагѡ дѣ́ла и҆
сло́ва дꙋшетлѣ́ннагѡ. Ѡ҆чи́сти, и҆ ѡ҆мы́й, и҆
оу҆краси́ мѧ: оу҆до́бри, вразꙋми́, и҆ просвѣти́
мѧ. Покажи́ мѧ твоѐ селéнïе є҆ди́нагѡ
дх҃а, и҆ не ктомꙋ̀ селéнïе грѣха̀. Да ꙗ҆́кѡ
твоегѡ̀ до́мꙋ вхо́домъ причащéнïѧ, ꙗ҆́кѡ
ѻ҆гна̀ менè бѣжи́тъ вса́къ ѕлодѣ́й, вса́ка
стра́сть. Мл҃твенники тебѣ̀ приношꙋ̀ вса̑
ст҃ы̑ѧ, чинонача́лïѧ же безпло́тныхъ,
предте́чꙋ твоегò, мꙋ́дрыѧ а҆пⷭ҇лы, къ си̑мъ
же твою̀ несквéрнꙋю чⷭ҇тꙋю мт҃рь, и҆́хже
мольбы̀, бл҃гоꙋтро́бне, прïими́, хрⷭ҇тè мо́й, и҆
сыномъ свѣ́та содѣ́лай твоегò слꙋжи́телѧ.
Ты́ бо є҆ди́нъ є҆сѝ и҆ ѡ҆сщ҃éнïе на́шихъ, бл҃же,
дꙋшъ и҆ свѣ́тлость, и҆ тебѣ̀ лѣпоподо́бнѡ,

but, rather, enter Thou into my members, into all my joints, my reigns, my heart. Burn up the thorns of all my sins. Purify my soul, sanctify my thoughts. Strengthen my substance together with my bones. Enlighten my simple five senses. Nail down the whole of me with Thy fear. Ever protect, preserve, and keep me from every soul-corrupting deed and word. Purify and cleanse, and adorn me; make me comely, give me understanding, and enlighten me. Show me to be the dwelling-place of Thy Spirit alone, and no longer the habitation of sin; that from me as Thine abode through the entry of Communion, every evil-doer, every passion, may flee as from fire. As intercessors I offer unto Thee all the saints, the commanders of the bodiless hosts, Thy Forerunner, the wise apostles, Thine undefiled pure Mother, whose entreaties do Thou accept, O my compassionate Christ, and make Thy servant a child of light. For Thou alone art our sanctification, O Good One,

ꙗ҆кѡ бг҃ꙋ и҆ влⷣцѣ, сла́вꙋ всѝ возсыла́емъ на всѧ́къ де́нь.

Мл҃тва и҆на́ѧ:

Тѣ́ло твоѐ ст҃о́е, гдⷭ҇и і҆и҃се хрⷭ҇тѐ бж҃е на́шъ, да бꙋ́детъ мѝ въ живо́тъ вѣ́чный, и҆ кро́вь твоѧ̀ чтⷭ҇на́ѧ во ѡ҆ставле́нїе грѣхѡ́въ: бꙋ́ди же мѝ бл҃годаре́нїе сїѐ въ ра́дость, здра́вїе и҆ весе́лїе, въ стра́шное же и҆ второ́е прише́ствїе твоѐ сподо́би мѧ̀ грѣ́шнаго ста́ти ѡ҆деснꙋ́ю сла́вы твоеѧ̀, мл҃твами пречⷭ҇тыѧ твоеѧ̀ мт҃ре и҆ всѣ́хъ ст҃ы́хъ.

Мл҃тва и҆на́ѧ, ко прест҃ѣ́й бцⷣѣ:

Прест҃а́ѧ влⷣчце бцⷣе, свѣ́те помрачѐнныѧ моеѧ̀ дꙋшѝ, наде́ждо, покро́ве, прибѣ́жище, ѹ҆тѣше́нїе, ра́дованїе моѐ: бл҃годарю́ тѧ, ꙗ҆кѡ сподо́била мѧ̀ є҆сѝ недосто́йнаго, причⷭ҇тника бы́ти пречⷭ҇тагѡ тѣ́ла, и҆ чтⷭ҇ныѧ кро́ве сн҃а твоегѡ̀. Но ро́ждшаѧ

and the radiance of our souls, and unto Thee
as God and Master, we all send up glory, as
is meet, every day.

Another Prayer:

O Lord Jesus Christ our God, may Thy
Holy Body be unto me for life eternal, and
Thy Precious Blood for the remission of
sins; and may this Eucharist be unto me for
joy, health, and gladness. And at Thy dread
Second Coming vouchsafe me, a sinner, to
stand at the right hand of Thy glory, through
the intercessions of Thy most pure Mother
and of all the saints.

Another Prayer, to the Most Holy Theotokos:

O most holy Lady Theotokos, light of my
darkened soul, my hope, protection, refuge,
consolation, my joy; I thank Thee that thou
hast vouchsafed me, who am unworthy, to
be a partaker of the most pure Body and precious Blood of thy Son. O Thou who gavest

и́стинный свѣ́тъ, просвѣтѝ моѧ̀ оу́мныѧ о́чи се́рдца: ꙗ́же исто́чникъ безсме́ртїѧ ро́ждшаѧ, ѡживотворѝ мѧ оу́мерцвле́ннаго грѣхо́мъ: ꙗ́же мл҃тиваго бг҃а любоблагоутро́бнаѧ мт҃и, помилꙋ́й мѧ̀, и да́ждь мѝ оу́миле́нїе, и сокрꙋше́нїе въ се́рдцѣ мое́мъ, и смире́нїе въ мы́слехъ мои́хъ, и воззва́нїе въ плѣне́нїихъ помышле́нїй мои́хъ: и сподо́би мѧ̀ до послѣ́днѧгѡ и́здыха́нїѧ, неѡсꙋжде́ннѡ прїнма́ти пречⷭ҇тыхъ та̑ннъ ѡсщ҃е́нїе, во исцѣле́нїе дꙋши́ же и тѣ́ла: и пода́ждь мѝ слё́зы покаѧ́нїѧ и исповѣ́данїѧ, во є́же пѣ́ти и сла́вити тѧ̀ во всѧ̑ дни живота̀ моегѡ̀, ꙗ́кѡ блгⷭ҇ове́нна и препросла́вленна єсѝ во вѣ́ки. Ами́нь.

Коне́цъ блгⷣа́рственныхъ мл҃твъ по ст҃ѣмъ причаще́нїи.

birth to the True Light, do Thou enlighten the spiritual eyes of my heart; Thou who gavest birth to the Source of Immortality, revive me who am dead in sin; Thou who art the lovingly-compassionate Mother of the merciful God, have mercy on me, and grant me compunction, and contrition in my heart, and humility in my thoughts, and the recall of my thoughts from captivity. And vouchsafe me until my last breath to receive without condemnation the sanctification of the most pure Mysteries, for the healing of both soul and body; and grant me tears of repentance and confession, that I may hymn and glorify thee all the days of my life, for blessed and most glorified art thou unto the ages. Amen.

The end of the thanksgiving prayers after Holy Communion.

Ѿпꙋ́сты пра́здникѡвъ и дневні́и

Ѿпꙋ́сты влады́чнихъ пра́здникѡвъ, глаго́лемїи въ вече́рню, во ꙋ́трєню и въ лїтꙋ́ргїю по чи́нꙋ.

На ржⷭ҇тво̀ хрⷭ҇то́во:

Иже въ верте́пѣ роди́выйсѧ, и въ ꙗ́слѣхъ возлегі́й, на́шегѡ ра́ди спⷭ҇е́нїѧ, хрⷭ҇то́съ и́стинный бг҃ъ на́шъ: и про́чее до конца̀.

На ѡбрѣ́занїе:

Иже во ѻсмы́й де́нь пло́тїю ѡбрѣ́затисѧ изво́ливый, на́шегѡ ра́ди спⷭ҇е́нїѧ, хрⷭ҇то́съ и́стинный бг҃ъ на́шъ:

На бгоѧвле́нїе:

Иже во їѻрда́нѣ крⷭ҇ти́тисѧ изво́ливый ѿ їѡа́нна, на́шегѡ ра́ди спⷭ҇е́нїѧ, хрⷭ҇то́съ и́стинный бг҃ъ на́шъ:

На срѣ́тенїе:

Иже во ѡбꙗ́тїихъ пра́веднагѡ сѷмеѡ́на носи́тисѧ изво́ливый, на́шегѡ ра́ди спⷭ҇е́нїѧ, хрⷭ҇то́съ и́стинный бг҃ъ на́шъ:

Festal and Daily Dismissals

Dismissals for Feasts of the Lord, which are said at Vespers, at Matins, and at the Liturgy, when indicated.

On the Nativity of Christ:
May Christ our true God, Who was born in a cave, and lay in a manger for our salvation,… and the rest unto the end.

On the Circumcision:
May Christ our true God, Who on the eighth day deigned to be circumcised for our salvation,…

On Theophany:
May Christ our true God, Who for our salvation deigned to be baptized by John in the Jordan,…

On the Meeting of the Lord:
May Christ our true God, Who for our salvation deigned to be carried in the arms of the Righteous Symeon,…

На преѡбраже́нїе:

И̑же на горѣ̀ ѳаво́рстѣй преѡбрази́выйсѧ во сла́вѣ пред ст҃ы́ми свои́ми ѹ̑ченикѝ и̑ а̑п҃лы, хр҃то́съ и̑́стинный бг҃ъ на́шъ:

Въ недѣ́лю цвѣ́тнꙋ́ю:

И̑же на жребѧ́ти ѻ̑́сли сѣ́сти и̑зво́ливый, на́шегѡ ра́ди сп҃се́нїѧ, хр҃то́съ и̑́стинный бг҃ъ на́шъ:

Въ тꙋ́ же недѣ́лю ве́чера:

Грѧды́й гд҃ь на во́льнꙋю стр҃ть, на́шегѡ ра́ди сп҃се́нїѧ, хр҃то́съ и̑́стинный бг҃ъ на́шъ:

Въ вели́кїй четверто́къ:

И̑же за превосходѧ́щꙋю бл҃гость пꙋ́ть добрѣ́йшїй смире́нїѧ показа́вый, внегда̀ ѹ̑мы́ти но́ги ѹ̑ченикѡ́въ, да́же и̑ до кр҃та̀ и̑ погребе́нїѧ снизше́дый на́мъ, хр҃то́съ и̑́стинный бг҃ъ на́шъ:

On Transfiguration:
May Christ our true God, Who on Mount Tabor was transfigured in glory before His holy disciples and apostles,…

On Palm Sunday:
May Christ our true God, Who for our salvation did deign to ride on the colt of an ass,…

On the same Sunday at Vespers:
May Christ our true God, the Lord Who for our salvation approacheth His voluntary Passion,…

On Great Thursday:
May Christ our true God, Who by His surpassing goodness did show the most excellent way of humility when He washed the feet of His disciples, and did condescend even unto the Cross and burial for us,…

Во ѿпу́стъ ст҃ы́хъ стрте́й:

И҆же ѡ҆плева́нїѧ, и҆ бїе́нїѧ, и҆ заꙋше́нїѧ, и҆ крⷭ҇тъ, и҆ сме́рть претерпѣ́вый за спⷭ҇е́нїе мі́ра, хрⷭ҇то́съ и҆́стинный бг҃ъ на́шъ:

Во ст҃ы́й и҆ вели́кїй пѧто́къ:

И҆же на́съ ра́ди человѣ́кѡвъ и҆ на́шегѡ ра́ди спⷭ҇е́нїѧ стра́шныѧ стрⷭ҇ти и҆ животворѧ́щїй крⷭ҇тъ и҆ во́льное погребе́нїе пло́тїю и҆зво́ливый, хрⷭ҇то́съ и҆́стинный бг҃ъ на́шъ:

Въ недѣ́лю па́схи и҆ во ст҃у́ю седми́цꙋ:

Хрⷭ҇то́съ воскрⷭ҇ый и҆з̾ ме́ртвыхъ, сме́ртїю сме́рть попра́вый и҆ сꙋ́щимъ во гробѣ́хъ живо́тъ дарова́вый, и҆́стинный бг҃ъ на́шъ:

На̀ вознесе́нїе:

И҆же во сла́вѣ вознесы́йсѧ ѿ на́съ на нб҃о и҆ ѡ҆десну́ю сѣ́дый бг҃а и҆ ѻ҆ц҃а̀, хрⷭ҇то́съ и҆́стинный бг҃ъ на́шъ:

At the dismissal of the Holy Passion
Gospels:
May Christ our true God, Who for the salvation of the world endured spitting, and
scourging, and buffeting, and the Cross, and
death,…

On Holy and Great Friday:
May Christ our true God, Who for us men
and for our salvation did deign to suffer the
dread Passion and the life-bearing Cross,
and voluntary burial in the flesh,…

On the Sunday of Pascha and during Bright
Week:
May Christ our true God, Who rose from
the dead, trampling down death by death
and on those in the tombs bestowing life,…

On Ascension:
May Christ our true God, Who in glory did
ascend from us into heaven and sit at the
right hand of God the Father,…

Въ недѣ́лю патдесѧ́тнꙋю:

И̂же въ видѣ́нїи ѻ̓гненныхъ ꙗ̂зы́къ съ нб҃сѐ низпосла́вый прест҃а́гѡ дх҃а на ст҃ы́ѧ своѧ̀ оу̓ченикѝ и̂ а̓пⷭ҇лы, хрⷭ҇то́съ и̂́стинный бг҃ъ на́шъ:

Въ тꙋ́ же недѣ́лю ве́чера:

И̂же ѿ ѻ̓́чихъ и̂ бж҃е́ственныхъ нѣ́дръ и̂сточи́вый себѐ, и̂ съ нб҃сѐ на зе́млю соше́дый, и̂ на́ше всѐ воспрїе́мый є̓стество̀, и̂ ѡ̓божи́вый є̀, по си́хъ же и̂ на нб҃са̀ па́ки возше́дый и̂ ѡ̓десно́ю сѣ́дый бг҃а и̂ ѻ̓ц҃а̀, бж҃е́ственнагѡ же и̂ ст҃а́гѡ, и̂ є̓диносꙋ́щнагѡ, и̂ є̓диноси́льнагѡ, и̂ є̓диносла́внагѡ, и̂ соприсносꙋ́щнагѡ дх҃а низпосла́вый на ст҃ы́ѧ своѧ̀ оу̓ченикѝ и̂ а̓пⷭ҇лы, и̂ си́мъ просвѣти́вый ѻ̓у̓бѡ и̂́хъ, тѣ́ми же всю̀ вселе́ннꙋю, хрⷭ҇то́съ и̂́стинный бг҃ъ на́шъ, моли́твами пречⷭ҇тыѧ и̂ пренепоро́чныѧ ст҃ы́ѧ своеѧ̀ мт҃ре, ст҃ы́хъ сла́вныхъ, прехва́льныхъ, бг҃опроповѣ́дникѡвъ и̂ дх҃оно́сныхъ а̓пⷭ҇лѡвъ и̂ всѣ́хъ ст҃ы́хъ,

On Pentecost Sunday:
May Christ our true God, Who sent down
from heaven the Most-holy Spirit in the
form of tongues of fire upon His holy disciples and apostles,...

On the same Sunday at Vespers:
May Christ our true God, Who did empty
Himself from the divine bosom of the
Father, and come down from the heavens
to the earth, and take upon Himself all our
nature, and deify it, and afterwards did
ascend again into the heavens and sit at the
right hand of God the Father, and did send
down upon His holy disciples and apostles
the Divine and Holy Spirit, one in essence,
one in power, one in glory, and co-everlast-
ing, and through Him did enlighten them,
and through them the whole world, through
the intercessions of His most pure and most
blameless Mother; of the holy, glorious,
most-praised preachers of God, the Spirit-

помилꙋетъ и̑ спсе́тъ на́съ, ꙗ҆́кѡ бл҃гъ и̑
чл҃вѣ́колю́бецъ.

Ѿпꙋ́сты дневни́н
во всю̀ седми́цꙋ, по ѻ҆бы́чаю ст҃ы́мъ
восто́чным црк҃ве.

Въ сꙋббѡ́тꙋ ве́чера и̑ недѣ́лю оу҆́тра:
Воскрⷭ҇ый и̑з ме́ртвыхъ хрⷭ҇то́съ и́стинный
бг҃ъ на́шъ, мл҃твами пречⷭ҇тыа своеа̀ мт҃ре,
ст҃ыхъ сла́вныхъ и̑ всехва́льныхъ а҆пⷭ҇лъ: [и̑
ст҃а́гѡ, є҆гѡ́же є҆́сть хра́мъ и̑ є҆гѡ́же є҆́сть
де́нь], ст҃ыхъ и̑ прв҃ныхъ бг҃оѻтє́цъ і̑ѡакі́ма
и̑ а҆́нны и̑ всѣ́хъ ст҃ы́хъ, помилꙋетъ и̑
спсе́тъ на́съ, ꙗ҆́кѡ бл҃гъ и̑ чл҃вѣ́колю́бецъ.

Въ недѣ́лю ве́чера и̑ въ понедѣ́льникъ
оу҆́тра:
Хрⷭ҇то́съ и́стинный бг҃ъ на́шъ, мл҃твами
пречⷭ҇тыа своеа̀ мт҃ре, предста́тельствы

bearing apostles; and of all the saints, have mercy on us and save us, for He is good and the Lover of mankind.

Daily Dismissals for all the week, according to the usage of the Holy Eastern Church.

On Saturday evening and Sunday morning:
May Christ our true God, Who rose from the dead, through the intercessions of His most pure Mother; of the holy, glorious, and all-praised apostles (and of the saint(s) whose temple it is and whose day it is); of the holy and Righteous Ancestors of God, Joachim and Anna; and of all the saints, have mercy on us and save us, for He is good and the Lover of mankind.

On Sunday evening and Monday morning:
May Christ our true God, through the intercessions of His most pure Mother, the

чⷮны́хъ нбⷭныхъ си́лъ безпло́тныхъ, стⷯыхъ
сла́вныхъ й всехва́льныхъ а҆пⷭлъ:

Въ понедѣ́льникъ ве́чера й во вто́рникъ
ѹ҆́тра:
Хрⷭто́съ и҆́стинный бг҃ъ на́шъ, мл҃твами
пречⷭтыл своѐѧ мт҃ре, чⷮна́гш сла́внагш
прⷪро́ка, предте́чи й крⷭти́телѧ і҆ша́нна,
стⷯыхъ сла́вныхъ й всехва́льныхъ а҆пⷭлъ: й
про́чаѧ.

Во вто́рникъ й въ четверто́къ ве́чера, въ
сре́дꙋ й въ пѧто́къ ѹ҆́тра:
Хрⷭто́съ и҆́стинный бг҃ъ на́шъ, мл҃твами
пречⷭтыл своѐѧ мт҃ре, си́лою чⷮна́гш й
животворѧ́щагш крⷭта̀, стⷯыхъ сла́вныхъ
й всехва́льныхъ а҆пⷭлъ: й про́чаѧ.

Въ сре́дꙋ ве́чера й въ четверто́къ ѹ҆́тра:
Хрⷭто́съ и҆́стинный бг҃ъ на́шъ, мл҃твами
пречⷭтыл своѐѧ мт҃ре, стⷯыхъ сла́вныхъ й

mediations of the honorable heavenly Bodiless Hosts, the intercessions of the holy, glorious, and all-praised apostles,…

On Monday evening and Tuesday
morning:
May Christ our true God, through the intercessions of His most pure Mother; of the
honorable, glorious Prophet, Forerunner,
and Baptist John; of the holy, glorious, and
all-praised apostles,…

On Tuesday and Thursday evenings, and
Wednesday and Friday mornings:
May Christ our true God, through the
intercessions of His most pure Mother; the
power of the precious and life-giving Cross,
the intercessions of the holy, glorious, and
all-praised apostles,…

On Wednesday evenings and Thursday
mornings:
May Christ our true God, through the
intercessions of His most pure Mother; of

всехва́льныхъ а҆пⷭ҇лъ, и҆́же во ст҃ы́хъ ѻ҆тца̀
на́шегѡ нїкола́а, а҆рхїепⷭ҇кпа мѷрлѷкı́йскихъ,
чꙋдотво́рца: и҆ про́чаѧ.

Въ пѧто́къ ве́чера и҆ въ сꙋббѡ́тꙋ оу҆́тра:
Хрⷭ҇то́съ и҆́стинный бг҃ъ на́шъ, мл҃твами
пречⷭ҇тыѧ своеѧ̀ мт҃ре, ст҃ы́хъ сла́вныхъ
и҆ всехва́льныхъ а҆пⷭ҇лъ, ст҃ы́хъ сла́вныхъ и҆
добропобѣ́дныхъ мч҃нкѡвъ, прпⷣбныхъ и҆
бг҃оно́сныхъ ѻ҆тє́цъ на́шихъ, [и҆ ст҃а́гѡ
хра́ма и҆ дне́], ст҃ы́хъ и҆ првⷣныхъ бг҃оѻтє́цъ
і҆ѡакı́ма и҆ а҆́нны и҆ всѣ́хъ ст҃ы́хъ, поми́лꙋетъ
и҆ сп҃се́тъ на́съ, ꙗ҆́кѡ бл҃гъ и҆ чл҃вѣколю́бецъ.

На ст҃ѣ́й лїтꙋргı́и во всю̀ седмицꙋ̀
быва́ютъ ѿпꙋ́сты, ꙗ҆́коже предписа́сѧ:
то́чїю по а҆пⷭ҇лѣ́хъ вставлѧ́етсѧ и҆ ст҃а́гѡ
и҆́мѧ, є҆гѡ́же є҆́сть лїтꙋргı́а, си́це:
И҆́же во ст҃ы́хъ ѻ҆тца̀ на́шегѡ і҆ѡа́нна,
а҆рхїепⷭ҇кпа кѡнстантı́на гра́да, златоꙋ́стагѡ.

the holy, glorious, and all-praised apostles, of our father among the saints, Nicholas the Wonderworker, archbishop of Myra in Lycia,…

On Friday evenings and Saturday mornings:

May Christ our true God, through the intercessions of His most pure Mother; of the holy, glorious, and all-praised apostles, of the holy, glorious, and victorious martyrs, of our holy and God-bearing fathers (and the saint(s) of the temple and the day), of the holy and Righteous Ancestors of God, Joachim and Anna, and of all the saints, have mercy on us and save us, for He is good and the Lover of mankind.

At the holy Liturgy through all the week the dismissals are as written above, except that after the apostles we insert also the name of the saint whose liturgy it is, thus: Of our father among the saints, John Chrysostom, archbishop of Constantinople.

Йлѝ: Васі́лїа вели́кагѡ, а҆рхїепкпа кеса́рїи каппадокі́йскїѧ.

Йлѝ: Григо́рїа двоесло́ва, па́пы ри́мскагѡ.

На повече́рїи, полꙋ́нощни́цѣ й пе́рвомъ часѣ̀ во все́й седми́цѣ быва́етъ ма́лый ѿпꙋ́стъ си́це:

Хрⷭ҇то́съ й҆́стинный бг҃ъ на́шъ, мл҃твами пречⷭ҇тыѧ своеѧ̀ мт҃ре, прпⷣбныхъ й бг҃оно́сныхъ ѻ҆те́цъ на́шихъ й всѣ́хъ ст҃ы́хъ, поми́лꙋетъ й спⷭ҇е́тъ на́съ, ꙗ҆́кѡ бл҃гъ й чл҃вѣколю́бецъ.

То́чїю въ недѣ́лю на полꙋ́нощни́цѣ й пе́рвомъ часѣ̀ прилага́етсѧ въ нача́лѣ:

Воскрⷭ҇ы́й и҆з̾ ме́ртвыхъ:

Вѣ́домо бꙋ́ди й ѡ҆ се́мъ, ꙗ҆́кѡ и҆дѣ́же є҆́сть хра́мъ спⷭ҇а хрⷭ҇та̀, ржⷭ҇тво̀, й҆лѝ бг҃оѧвле́нїе, й҆лѝ вознесе́нїе, й҆ про́чаѧ, въ седми́чномъ ѿпꙋ́стѣ не возглаша́ютсѧ пра́здничные

Or: Basil the Great, archbishop of Caesarea in Cappadocia.

Or: Gregory the Dialogist, the Pope of Rome.

At Compline, the Midnight Office, and the First Hour throughout the week, the Lesser Dismissal is done thus:

May Christ our true God, through the intercessions of His most pure Mother, of our holy and God-bearing fathers, and of all the saints, have mercy on us and save us, for He is good and the Lover of mankind.

But on Sundays, at the Midnight Office and the First Hour, the following is appended to the beginning:

May Christ our true God, Who rose from the dead,...

Be it known also concerning this, that where there be a temple dedicated to Christ the Saviour, the Nativity, or the Theophany, or the Ascension, etc., at the weekday dismissal

Ѿпꙋ́сты, то́чїю возглаша́етсѧ пра́здничный Ѿпꙋ́стъ въ де́нь пра́здника и̑ до Ѿда́нїѧ: а̑ во ве́сь го́дъ то́кмѡ: Хрⷭ҇то́съ и̑́стинный бг҃ъ на́шъ: и̑ про́чаѧ по дню̀.

the festal dismissals are not said, but only on the day of the feast and until the apodosis (leave-taking) is the festal dismissal said; but during the entire year only **May Christ our true God**: and the rest according to the day of the week.

Прошéнїѧ на рáзныѧ потрéбы:

Е҆щѐ мóлимсѧ тебѣ̀, гд҃у бг҃у нáшемꙋ, є҆́же оу҆слы́шатисѧ глáсꙋ молéнїѧ нáшегѡ, и҆ мл҃твѣ, и҆ поми́ловати рабѡ́въ твои́хъ и҆́мк: бл҃годáтїю и҆ щедрóтами твои́ми, и҆ и҆спóлнити всѧ̀ прошéнїѧ и҆́хъ, и҆ прости́ти и҆́мъ всѧ̀ согрѣшéнїѧ вѡ́льнаѧ и҆ невѡ́льнаѧ: бл҃гопрїѧ́тнымъ же бы́ти мольбáмъ и҆ ми́лостынамъ и҆́хъ пред престóломъ вл҃чествїѧ твоегѡ̀, и҆ покры́ти и҆́хъ ѿ врáгъ види́мыхъ и҆ неви́димыхъ, ѿ всѧ́кїѧ напáсти, бѣды̀ и҆ скóрби, и҆ недꙋ́гѡвъ и҆збáвити, и҆ подáти здрáвїе съ долгодéнствїемъ: рцéмъ всѝ, гд҃и, оу҆слы́ши и҆ поми́лꙋй.

Ли́къ: Гд҃и, поми́лꙋй, три́жды.

Призри, вл҃ко чл҃вѣколю́бче, ми́лтивымъ ти̑ ѻ҆́комъ на рабѡ́въ твои́хъ и҆́мк: и҆ оу҆слы́ши молéнїѧ нáша съ вѣ́рою приносѧ́маѧ, ꙗ҆́кѡ сáмъ рéклъ є҆сѝ: всѧ̀

Petitions for Various Needs

Again we pray Thee, O Lord our God, that Thou wouldst hearken unto the voice of our supplication and prayer, and have mercy on Thy servants N. through Thy grace and compassions, and fulfill all their petitions, and pardon them all transgressions voluntary and involuntary, let their prayers and alms be acceptable before the throne of Thy dominion, and protect them from enemies visible and invisible, from every temptation, harm, and sorrow, and deliver them from diseases, and grant them health and length of days: let us all say, O Lord, hearken and have mercy.

Choir: Lord, have mercy (thrice).

Look down, O Master, Lover of mankind, with Thy merciful eye, upon Thy servants N. and hearken unto our supplication which is offered with faith, for Thou Thyself hast

є҆ли́ка молѧ́щесѧ про́сите, вѣ́рꙋйте, ꙗ҆́кѡ
прїи́мете, и҆ бꙋ́детъ ва́мъ, и҆ па́ки: проси́те
и҆ да́стсѧ ва́мъ: сегѡ̀ ра́ди и҆ мы̀, а҆́ще и҆
недосто́йнїи, ѹ҆пова́юще на ми́лость твою̀,
про́симъ: пода́ждь бл҃гость твою̀ рабѡ́мъ
твои́мъ и҆̀мк҃: и҆ и҆спо́лни бл҃га̑ѧ жела̑нїѧ
и҆̀хъ, ми́рнѡ же и҆ ти́хѡ въ здра́вїи, и҆
долгодє́нствїи всѧ̑ дни̑ и҆̀хъ соблюдѝ: рцє́мъ
всѝ, ско́рѡ ѹ҆слы́ши и҆ ми́лостивнѡ поми́лꙋй.
Ли́къ: Гд҃и, поми́лꙋй, три́жды.

Е҆ще́ мо́лимсѧ ѡ҆ предстоѧ́щихъ лю́дехъ,
ѡ҆жида́ющихъ ѿ тебє̀ вели́кїѧ и҆ бога́тыѧ
мл҃ти, за всю̀ бра́тїю, и҆ за всѧ̑ хрⷭ҇тїа́ны.
Ли́къ: Гд҃и, поми́лꙋй, три́жды.

Е҆ктенїа̀ ѡ҆ болѧ́щихъ:

Врачꙋ̀ дꙋ́шъ и҆ тѣле́съ, со ѹ҆милє́нїемъ въ
се́рдцѣ сокрꙋше́нномъ къ тебѣ̀ припа́даемъ,

said: "All things whatsoever ye shall ask in prayer, believe that ye shall receive, and it will be done unto you," and again: "Ask, and it shall be given to you." Therefore we, though we be unworthy, yet hoping in thy mercy, ask: bestow Thy kindness upon Thy servants N. and fulfill their good desires, preserve them all their days peacefully and calmly in health and length of days: let us all say, quickly hearken and graciously have mercy.

Choir: Lord, have mercy (thrice).

Again we pray for the people here present that await of Thee great and abundant mercy, for all the brethren, and for all Christians.

Choir: Lord, have mercy (thrice).

Litany for the Sick:

O Physician of souls and bodies, with compunction and broken hearts we fall down

и҆ стенѧ́ще вопїе́мъ ти̑: и҆сцѣли̑ болѣ́зни,
оу҆врачꙋ́й стра́сти дꙋ́шъ и҆ тѣле́съ рабѡ́въ
твои́хъ и҆́мк: и҆ прости̑ и҆̀мъ, ꙗ҆́кѡ бл҃госе́рдъ,
всѧ̑ прегрѣше́нїѧ, вѡ́льнаѧ и҆ невѡ́льнаѧ,
и҆ ско́рѡ воздви́гни ѿ ѻ҆дра̀ болѣ́зни,
мо́лимъ ти сѧ, оу҆слы́ши и҆ поми́лꙋй.

Ли́къ: Гд҃и, поми́лꙋй, три́жды.

Не хотѧ́й сме́рти грѣ́шныхъ, но е҆́же
ѡ҆брати́тисѧ и҆ живы̑мъ и҆̀мъ бы́ти,
пощади̑ и҆ поми́лꙋй рабѡ́въ твои́хъ и҆́мк:
мл҃тиве, запрети̑ болѣ́зни, ѿста́ви всю̀
стра́сть, и҆ ве́сь недꙋ́гъ, оу҆толи̑ зи́мꙋ и҆
ѻ҆́гнь, и҆ простри̑ крѣ́пкꙋю твою̀ рꙋ́кꙋ, и҆
ꙗ҆́коже і҆а́ірову дще́рь ѿ ѻ҆дра̀ болѣ́зни
воздви́гни, и҆ здра́выхъ предста́ви, мо́лимъ
ти сѧ, оу҆слы́ши и҆ поми́лꙋй.

Ли́къ: Гд҃и, поми́лꙋй, три́жды.

Ѻ҆гненнꙋ́ю болѣ́знь петро́вой те́щи
прикоснове́нїемъ твои́мъ и҆сцѣли́вый, и҆
нынѣ лю́тѣ стра́ждꙋщихъ рабѡ́въ твои́хъ
и҆́мк: болѣ́знь бл҃госе́рдїемъ твои́мъ
и҆сцѣли̑, здра́вїе и҆̀мъ ско́рѡ подава́ѧ,

before Thee, and groaning we cry unto
Thee: heal the sicknesses, heal the passions
of the soul and body of Thy servants N., and
pardon them, for Thou art kindhearted, all
transgressions, voluntary and involuntary,
and quickly raise them up from the bed of
sickness, we pray thee, hearken and have
mercy.

Choir: Lord, have mercy (thrice).

O Thou Who desirest not the death of sinners, but rather that they should return to
Thee, and live: Spare and have mercy on
Thy servants N., O Merciful One, banish
sickness, drive away all passion, and all ail-
ments, assuage chill and fever, and stretch
forth Thy mighty arm and, as Thou didst
raise up Jairus' daughter from the bed of
sickness, restore them to health, we pray
Thee, hearken and have mercy.

Choir: Lord, have mercy (thrice).

O Thou Who by thy touch didst heal Peter's
mother-in-law who was sick with fever: do

прилѣ́жнѡ мо́лимъ ти сѧ, исто́чниче
цѣльба́мъ, оу҆слы́ши и҆ поми́лꙋй.

Ли́къ: Гд҃и, поми́лꙋй, три́жды.

Є҆ще́ мо́лимсѧ гдꙋ бг҃ꙋ на́шемꙋ, ѡ҆ є҆́же
оу҆слы́шати гла́съ моле́нїѧ на́съ грѣ́шныхъ,
и҆ поми́ловати рабѡ́въ свои́хъ, и҆́мⷬ҇къ: и҆
покры́ти и҆̀хъ ѿ всѧ́кїѧ ско́рби, бѣды̀,
гнѣ́ва и҆ нꙋ́жды, и҆ ѿ всѧ́кїѧ болѣ́зни
дꙋше́вныѧ и҆ тѣле́сныѧ, дарова́ти же
и҆̀мъ здра́вїе съ долгоде́нствїемъ, рце́мъ
всѝ: ско́рѡ оу҆слы́ши и҆ ма́тивнѡ поми́лꙋй.

Ли́къ: Гд҃и, поми́лꙋй, три́жды.

Ѡ пꙋтеше́ствꙋющихъ:

Стѡпы̀ человѣ́ческїѧ и҆справлѧ́ѧй, гд҃и,
при́зри ма́тивнѡ на рабы̀ твоѧ̀ и҆́мⷬ҇къ,
и҆ прости́въ и҆̀мъ всѧ́кое прегрѣше́нїе,

Thou now, in Thy loving-kindness, heal Thy terribly-suffering servants of their malady, quickly granting them health, we diligently pray Thee, O Fount of healing, hearken and have mercy.

Choir: Lord, have mercy (thrice).

Again we pray to the Lord our God, that He may hearken unto the voice of the supplications of us sinners, and have mercy on His servants N., and protect them from all tribulation, harm, wrath, and necessity, and from every sickness of soul and body, granting them health with length of days, let us all say, quickly hearken and graciously have mercy.

Choir: Lord, have mercy (thrice).

For Those Who Journey:

O Lord, Who dost guide the footsteps of mankind, graciously look upon Thy servants N., and pardoning them every trans-

во́льное же и нево́льное, бл҃гослови̑ бл҃го́е
намѣ́ренїе совѣ́та и҆́хъ, и҆ и҆схо́ды и҆ входы
со пꙋтьше́ствїемъ и҆спра́ви, прилѣ́жно
мо́лимъ ти сѧ, оу҆слы́ши и҆ помилꙋ́й.
Ли́къ: Гдⷭ҇и, поми́лꙋй, три́жды.

І҆ѡ́сифа ѿ ѡ҆ѕлобле́нїѧ бра́тїй ѥ҆гѡ̀
пресла́внѡ свободи́вый Гдⷭ҇и, и҆ во ѥ҆гѵ́петъ
того̀ наста́вивый, и҆ бл҃гослове́нїемъ твое́ѧ
бл҃гости во все́мъ бл҃гополꙋ́чна сотвори́вый:
и҆ си́хъ рабѡ́въ твои́хъ пꙋтьше́ствовати
хотѧ́щихъ бл҃гослови̑, и҆ ше́ствїе и҆́хъ
безмѧте́жно и҆ бл҃гополꙋ́чно сотвори̑,
мо́лимъ ти сѧ, оу҆слы́ши и҆ помилꙋ́й.
Ли́къ: Гдⷭ҇и, поми́лꙋй, три́жды.

Бл҃годаре́нїе ѡ҆ полꙋче́нїи прошє́нїѧ:

Бл҃годарѧ́ще со стра́хомъ и҆ трепе́томъ ꙗ҆́кѡ
раби̑ непотре́бнїи, твоемꙋ̀ бл҃гоꙋтро́бїю, сп҃се
и҆ вл҃ко на́шъ Гдⷭ҇и, ѡ҆ твои́хъ бл҃годѣѧ́нїихъ,
ꙗ҆́же и҆злїѧ́лъ є҆сѝ и҆зоби́льнѡ на рабѣ́хъ
твои́хъ, и҆ припа́даемъ и҆ славосло́вїе тебѣ̀

gression, both voluntary and involuntary, bless the good intention of their counsel, and guide their goings out and comings in on the journey, we earnestly pray Thee, hearken and have mercy.

Choir: Lord, have mercy (thrice).

O Lord, Who didst most gloriously deliver Joseph from the animosity of his brethren, and didst lead him to Egypt, and through the blessing of Thy goodness didst make him to prosper in all things: Bless also these Thy servants who desire to travel, and cause their journey to be safe and tranquil, we pray Thee, hearken and have mercy.

Choir: Lord, have mercy (thrice).

Thanksgiving for Petitions Granted:

Giving thanks with fear and trembling, as unprofitable servants, unto Thy loving-kindness, O Lord our Saviour and Master, for Thy benefits which Thou hast poured out

ꙗ́кѡ бг҃у прино́симъ, и҆ ѹ҆мине́ннѡ вопїе́мъ: и҆зба́ви ѿ всѣ́хъ бѣ́дъ рабы̀ твоѧ̀, и҆ всегда̀, ꙗ҆́кѡ мл҃тивъ, и҆спо́лни во бл҃ги́хъ жела́нїе всѣ́хъ на́съ, прилѣ́жнѡ мо́лимъ ти сѧ, ѹ҆слы́ши и҆ поми́луй.

Ли́къ: Гд҃и, поми́луй, три́жды.

Ꙗ҆́коже ны́нѣ мл҃тивнѡ ѹ҆слы́шалъ є҆сѝ мл҃твы рабѡ́въ твои́хъ, гд҃и, и҆ ꙗ҆ви́лъ є҆сѝ на ни́хъ бл҃гоѹтро́бїе чл҃вѣколю́бїѧ твоегѡ̀, си́це и҆ въ пре́днѧѧ не презира́ѧ, и҆спо́лни во сла́ву твою̀ всѧ̀ бл҃га́ѧ хотѣ́нїѧ вѣ́рныхъ твои́хъ, и҆ ꙗ҆вѝ всѣ̑мъ на́мъ бога́тую мл҃ть твою̀, всѧ̑ на́мъ согрѣше́нїѧ презира́ѧ: мо́лимъ ти сѧ, ѹ҆слы́ши и҆ поми́луй.

Ли́къ: Гд҃и, поми́луй, три́жды.

abundantly on Thy servants, we fall down in worship and offer a doxology unto Thee as God, and fervently cry aloud to Thee: deliver Thou Thy servants from all misfortune, and, as Thou art merciful, always fulfill the desires of us all unto good, we diligently pray Thee, hearken and have mercy.

Choir: Lord, have mercy (thrice).

In that Thou now hast mercifully hearkened unto the prayers of Thy servants, O Lord, and hast manifested upon us the tender compassion of Thy love for mankind, so also, in time to come, disdaining us not, do Thou fulfill, unto Thy glory, all good desires of Thy faithful, and show unto all of us Thine abundant mercy, disregarding all our iniquities, we pray Thee, hearken and have mercy.

Choir: Lord, have mercy (thrice).